J

"

r

r

in 1992. His playing career stretched from 1992 until 1998, during which time he notched up 60 caps. He was part of the successful 1993 team which won every trophy on offer including the Super 10, Currie Cup, Lion Cup and M-Net trophy. In 1997 he was awarded the national club championship player of the year, scoring 24 tries in 14 matches, also being the highest point scorer of the tournament. In 1998 he retired from the professional game. He has an honours degree in Financial Management from RAU (University of Johannesburg), is a Certified Financial Planner, a member of the Financial Planning Institute, and now runs his own medical-aid brokerage.

THE
GIRLFRIEND'S
GUIDE
TO
RUGBY

JACO LOUW

Illustrated by Derrick Nesbit

30° South Publishers

Published in 2008 by 30° South Publishers (Pty) Ltd.
28, Ninth Street, Newlands
Johannesburg 2092, South Africa
www.30degreessouth.co.za
info@30degreessouth.co.za

Illustrations by Derrick Nesbit

Design and origination by 30° South Publishers (Pty) Ltd.
Printed and bound by Pinetown Printers, Durban

ISBN: 978-0-620395-41-0

For Kobus, Lynette and Oom Alec

contents

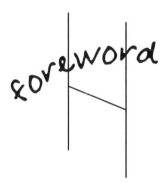

Rugby's shortest forward ... ag, I mean foreword!

Rugby has been described in many ways, but none as accurate as 'a hooligan's game played by gentlemen'. The game is a lot like life; it is full of passion, blood, sweat and tears.

Rugby makes grown men cry or act in strange ways ... well, this according to their wives or girlfriends! What these female 'critics' do not realize or understand is how involved and intense this great game really is.

There are so many rules and laws interpreted by referees in so many different ways. There is also club, province and country to support, yet so little time in which to do them all justice.

Now, for the first time, a book—no wait, a guide—has been created by a former player, Jaco Louw, to inform, educate and provide insight into the world of rugby, especially to the 'critics'.

Very important aspects of the game are dealt with, like:

- Why men get so passionate about rugby
- Why rugby is as important to men as shopping is to women
- Insight into the new ELVs
- What women miss out on by not joining or supporting the man or men in their lives for a game of rugby

In fact, women must understand; rugby is not a matter of life and death. Oh no, it is far more important than that!

By reading this book, women will discover a new world opening up to them, will understand their men better, and see there is more to rugby than merely spotting 'talent' from the stands.

For 80 minutes, once a week, a woman can spend quality time with the man in her life, showing support for and bonding with him, while both of them sport the colours of their team painted onto their faces. Think of the converse; this will allow men to better understand the daily arduous task of applying make-up to improve their looks!

The classified information contained in this book will, once and for all, pave the way for better understanding and compromise between men and women when it comes to rugby.

I would go as far as to say that my advice to women out there is as follows: if you want to cement the hold on your man, read this book, study this book, memorize this book.

To the men out there, this book is a must for the girl in your life. It will put an end to the nagging from them, the begging from you and make you the man among men once more!

This book is also great value for money because it can be passed down to all the other, younger female members of the family, so they too can understand their men better … even before they have met them!

You will love this book. I know my wife will … because I say so!

Kobus Wiese
December 2008

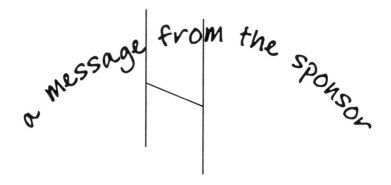

a message from the sponsor

Lefatshe Technologies is extremely proud to be associated with Jaco Louw and his project: *The Girlfriend's Guide to Rugby* and the development work that he is doing in the form of clinics in underprivileged communities. Sport is a wonderful way of instilling discipline and building character in young people as it simultaneously breaks down the walls that have traditionally divided us.

We loved the concept of the book and believe that it is a fantastic way to introduce the fairer sex to the great game of rugby, the religion of masses of warm-blooded South African men. We know that you will enjoy the book too!

We congratulate Jaco on his achievement in completing the book, and thank him for considering us worthy of being associated with this project. It has been our absolute pleasure to be the sponsor. Now even I will know the difference between a ruck and a maul!

Noedine Isaacs-Mpulo
CEO: Lefatshe Technologies

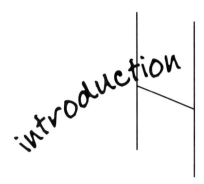

introduction

"... I can't wait for Saturday! There are three rugby games in the morning, starting at 07:30 and finishing at 14:00; then there's the big game at 17:00 and another one at 19:00! We can start off with a champagne breakfast at Kwota's house, quickly run to the shops with Sandy from 14:00 to 15:00 and then start warming up for the big one ..." While this might well be what Barry is thinking—and maybe even planning—he will never dare put it to Sandy this way, because that could cause more mayhem than letting Monica Lewinsky loose in the White House again.

Sandy can't wait for Saturday either. She and Barry can have a nice sleep-in, then have breakfast at the tea-garden down the road. After that, she will take him to the Louis Vuitton store in the new mall to show him the handbag she wants for her birthday, and perhaps at the same time he can help her pick out a dress and shoes to go with it. Festooned by now with pricey, rejected apparel and looking like a washing line, he might as well also help her choose something to wear to Chris and Lucy's wedding. Then perhaps they can top off the afternoon with some shamelessly indulgent ice-cream at Häagen-Dazs and a cappuccino at one of those little coffee shops where they have all the latest fashion magazines so she can compare what she bought with the outfits worn by the vapid, anorexic wraiths in the glossy pages and decide whether it needs to go back.

Oh, and if they're quick, they might just be home in time for the second half of the 'big game' he's been banging on about, which he can watch right after he has fixed her dishwasher and put a new plug on her hairdryer! Perfect!

She wouldn't say this to him either, because it may just prickle the rebel in him enough to stay home and watch rugby all day! So, master campaigner that she is, she will only mention the breakfast, and poor predictable Barry will tag along excitedly, like a dog will follow its master as he goes to put the bowl by the back door.

They'll gobble a heavenly breakfast, and then the con begins …

"Sweetheart, I just want to run into Louis Vuitton quickly …"

The next five or six hours are pure pain, torture and suffering. The self-control required in these situations can be equated to that of a monk at Teasers.

This dilemma is one I have watched and experienced throughout my adult life. We all know how we'd *prefer* to spend our free time, but because we have partners and want to spend time with them too, we compromise—which means a bit more shopping for the guys and a bit more rugby for the girls!

This little book aims to make that compromise a bit easier for the girlfriends, wives and even male friends who are not into rugby (yes; unbelievably there *are* such people). Besides a good chuckle here and there, this easy-reference guide will teach novice and expert alike the ins-and-outs of this wonderful game. Who knows … sooner or later, *she* might be the one rushing through the shopping to get home in time for the game!

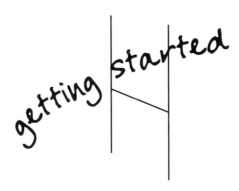

getting started

Get yourself a team!
Use the following criteria:

- Where were you born?
- Where do you live now?
- Which team does your boyfriend/husband support?
- Which team has the nicest jerseys?
- Which team has the best-looking players?

Any of these questions can help you decide who you should support. It may be wise to choose the same team as your other half, but if you like to stir a bit, pick their traditional rivals. Even I get bored watching two teams play when I have no emotional investment in either. It's a bare essential … you have to have a team!

Check the schedule
The fixtures for 2009 are listed in Appendix 2 of this book. Make a note of when your team is playing.

Buy your favourite drink

It is important that you feel relaxed and calm before the start of the match. Be sure that your glass is full, that the bottle is next to you, and that you have an unobstructed view of the screen.

Keep this book close by

The first time you attempt to follow a game, keep *The Girlfriend's Guide* handy. Every time the whistle blows, listen to what Reffie says and look it up. After the first half, you will already have a clearer idea what's going on.

Let the emotion come!

If your team makes a silly mistake, get angry! If they are worthy of your support, you expect a high-quality game from them. If the referee seems to be biased against your team, swear at him—it helps!

Meet the characters

Barry

He is Joe-sixpack, loves sport, loves a party and loves his girlfriend but not necessarily in that order. He has a middle-management job with a middle-management salary, and is more concerned with having enough to drink and eat during a rugby match than having a decent couch to sit on while doing so! He does not understand shopping beyond buying beer and food and, at a push, a new pair of jeans.

Sandy

She is the girl next door, and Barry's girlfriend. She is slightly naïve, but can turn a few heads when she goes out. She loves shopping and accessorizing. Having a good handbag and a fancy pair of shoes

is far more important than eating and partying. She likes socializing, but cannot comprehend why Barry's parties never end before the sun comes up. She has tolerated Barry's passion for sport; in fact she has even enjoyed the hype and excitement when there is a really big game on. But she has no clue what actually happens on the field, nor does she really care.

Kwota

His real name is Jabu. He is Barry's best friend, and they work for the same company. He is a really laid-back person and loves sport, rap music and bling. His favourite saying is 'Chill, bru'. Hanging out with Barry, watching sports and drinking beer is Kwota's Utopia.

Reffie

He is that irritating little man who blows a whistle every time the fun starts. Anything that is not 100 per cent correct, and Reffie stops the game. He has the authority to intervene, and loves using it. He means well, but sometimes he is just a little too much. He doesn't miss a trick, and the players are aware that they have to watch every move they make because Reffie always sees them!

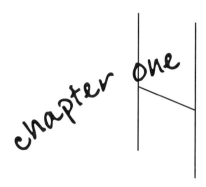

chapter one

The basics of the game

The ball

The ball used in Rugby Union, or rugby, is egg-shaped and white in colour. The shape makes it difficult to judge which way it will bounce when it falls, and a little harder to catch and kick than a round ball. The modern-day rugby ball has been designed not to absorb any water if it gets wet. This ensures that it does not get heavier in wet weather, like the older leather balls did. It does have the added disadvantage, though, that when it gets wet it becomes more slippery than a nipple in an oil-wrestling contest, and as hard to handle.

The pitch

Rugby is played on a grass pitch, (other than in Potchefstroom and Kimberley, where it is mostly played on gravel). The lines that border the length of the pitch are called 'touch-lines', and those bordering the width are called 'dead-ball lines'.

If you start walking from the one dead-ball line towards the other, the next solid horizontal line is the try-line. An H-shaped goal-post is planted in the middle of this line. The area between the try-line and the dead-ball line is called the in-goal area. 22-metres further on, you will encounter the 22-metre line, followed 28 metres later by the halfway line. Ten metres before you reach the halfway line, you will see a broken or dotted line. This is called the 10-metre line. The other half of the field is a mirror-image of the half you've just walked (as illustrated by the sketch below). The pitch measures 100 metres from try-line to try-line, and is 50 metres wide.

The teams

The game is contested between two teams, each consisting of 15 players and 7 substitutes. No more than 15 players per team are allowed to take the field at any given time. This means that 15 guys will play, while the seven 'spare' guys sit next to the field and wait for their chance to play, loudly confident that they could do much better than the imbecile who's on the field in their position at that moment. These reserve troops get to play when someone on the pitch is injured and can't continue, or when the coach decides to take off one of the 15 players and replace him with one of the seven on the bench.

Time

The game is played in two halves of 40 minutes each. Half-time is about ten minutes, after which the teams swop sides. If the game is stopped because of injury, substitution or a pending television referee's decision, the official timekeeper stops the clock. The referee on the field will signal to him when to start the clock again. He will do this by raising an open hand and saying … you guessed it … "Time on!"

Now girls, I know you are already doing the arithmetic … if the game is 40 minutes a side, with ten minutes' break, and allowing some time for injury stoppages, it can never take longer than 100 minutes. Why is it then, that when the game starts at 5:00, Barry doesn't get home till well after two in the morning? Surely he could be back by 18:30 or 19:00?

Remember, there is a lot of thinking to do after the game. We sit down and analyze every move, and decide who should be dropped and who should be promoted. There is also serious consideration for the traffic and how unsafe it would be to leave straight after the game (the likelihood of a roadblock at that hour is very high). So if we take a little longer than the actual time of the match, it is really to make sure that we get home safely and don't spoil your evening by talking about the game all night, or disturb your chick flick by calling you away from a vital scene. We have discovered you are far less understanding of the latter.

The object of the game

Like most other games, the object of the game is for one team to score more points than the other. There are four ways to score points in rugby:

- Scoring a try   5 points
- Conversion kick   2 points
- Penalty kick   3 points
- Drop kick   3 points

Scoring a try

A try is scored when a player from one team manages to carry the ball over the try-line of the other team and grounds it. The defending team will do everything in their power to stop the attackers from doing so. If this is the ultimate goal of the game, why is it called a 'try' once you've achieved it? No, I can't tell you why a doctor or a lawyer starts to 'practise' once they are qualified, but there is an explanation for the 'try' in rugby. Way back in history, when the game was in its infancy, the only way to score points was to kick the ball over the H-shaped goal-posts. The rules dictated that you had to carry the ball over the try-line and ground it before you were allowed to kick at goal. Therefore you scored a 'try', because this earned you the right to try and kick the ball over the posts. The powers-that-were obviously realized that it was far more entertaining to watch the teams battle to get the ball over the line than kicking for goal. They started off by giving teams one point for a try and, as the game developed, increased its value. Today it is worth five points.

Possession of the ball is a very important part of the game. Possession on its own does not mean points, but you can't score points without the ball. The team with the ball in hand may pass it, kick it or run with it.

If a player passes the ball to a teammate, this teammate must be behind him when he receives the ball. The ball may *never* go forward from the ball-carrier's hands, whether from a pass or accidentally dropping it. This will result in a scrum being awarded to the defending side, and hence possession will be lost (*see* Chapter 3).

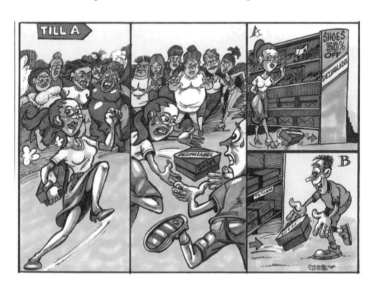

The defending team will try and stop the attackers by tackling the player with the ball, forcing him to drop the ball, or make some other mistake. Tackling an opponent basically means you physically stop the guy with the ball by grabbing his legs and diving into him, pulling him to the ground and falling on him, or any other way you can think of to get him down—as long as you do *not* make contact with anything above his  shoulders and you don't pick him up and drive his head into the ground. Either of these offences will lead to a penalty being awarded to the opposing side (*see* Chapter 3).

The conversion kick

A conversion kick is only awarded once a try has been scored. This is when the player places the ball on a kicking tee (some players even use sand) and attempts to kick it between the H-shaped goalposts, over the crossbar. If he is successful, two points will be added to the score. A conversion kick needs to be taken in line from the spot where the ball was grounded when the try was scored. (This is why you often see players running as close as possible to the goalposts before grounding the ball, even after crossing the try-line.) The kicker can decide how far forward or back he wants to place the ball. The kicker does not have to be the same person as the one who scored the try. The defending team has to stand behind their own try-line while the kicker lines up the kick; but they are allowed to charge him as soon as he starts his run-up towards the ball.

It is obvious why scoring tries is the best way of accumulating points. The try earns you five points and automatically gives your kicker the opportunity to add another two with the conversion. With the skill levels of modern-day kickers, most tries are worth seven points.

The penalty kick

A penalty is awarded for various offences (*see* Chapter 4). Once a penalty is awarded, the kicker and captain of the side will decide whether the spot where the penalty has been awarded is close enough to the goal-posts for the kicker to kick the ball over the crossbar between the posts. Once again he will use a kicking tee or sand to place the ball, and attempt to kick it over. If he is successful, three points will be added to his team's score. The defending team is not allowed to charge him when he is attempting a penalty kick.

The drop kick

This is when a player drops the ball onto the ground before kicking it through the goal-posts over the crossbar. This is very difficult to do, as it happens while the ball is in play—meaning that the defending team is chasing the player with the ball, who then needs to steady himself, drop the ball to the ground and kick it through the posts while in motion. Who can forget the drop kick by Joel Stransky in extra time of the 1995 Rugby World Cup which sank the All Blacks and won the game for the Springboks? A successful drop kick is worth three points.

Summary

- Rugby is a game played with an egg-shaped ball on a grass pitch, 100 metres in length from try-line to try-line, and 50 metres in width.

- Each team consists of 15 players and 7 substitutes.

- The object of the game is to score points by crossing the opposing team's try-line and grounding the ball.

- Points can also be scored by kicking the ball over the crossbar between the posts in one of the following ways:

  - a conversion kick (after a try has been scored).
  - a penalty kick (awarded by the referee).
  - a drop kick (executed while the ball is in play).

- Even though the game lasts for 80 minutes, watching it may take a little longer!

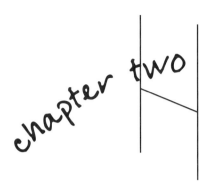

Players and officials

Officials and their roles

The man with the whistle is the main official (Reffie). He is called the referee, and he is assisted by two other officials on the park, called assistant referees. (Previously they were called touch-judges.)

Together they are affectionately referred to as the 'three blind mice'. Although this often appears to be the case, spare a thought for the man in the middle. Refereeing must be one of the most thankless jobs there is. No matter how good he is, somebody is going to hate him for a decision he makes. I can personally say I have never lost a game where we had a good referee … Of course this is said in jest, but one of the referee's hardest duties is to control 30 large men, revved up and weeping testosterone from the pores. Watching rugby on television gives no sense of the pressure players put on the referee. Remembering that many of the players are legends in their own time, chirping the referee and advising him on decisions and how to referee the game becomes part of their make-up. It takes a very strong character to pull this off.

One of the funniest chirps on a rugby field happened in an Australian test match. The referee blew his whistle very hard and said "I've had enough! There are 30 referees on this field!" to which the Australian captain, Nick Farr-Jones, replied as he jogged past: "Problem is, you're not even in the top ten!"

The assistant referees, who are also qualified referees, each patrol one of the touch-lines. They carry flags in their hands and one of their duties is to raise the flag when the ball goes out of play. They have to run along the touch-lines and raise the flag at the point where the ball, or any body part of a player carrying the ball, crosses the touch-line. This will result in a lineout (*see* Chapter 3). The lineout throw will be awarded to the team who *did not* carry or kick the ball into touch. The exception to this is a penalty kick. If a team kicks the ball into touch from a penalty kick, they will also throw the ball into the lineout.

Should the kicker of the team decide to have a kick at goal from a penalty, the assistant referees will run around and stand behind the goal-post that the kicker is aiming at. It is their duty to judge whether the ball goes over the crossbar between the uprights. If the kick goes over, they will raise their flags. If it misses, they will keep the flags down and wave them horizontally to their bodies.

The assistant referees are in radio contact with the referee, and

can advise him on any mistakes that he may have missed. Foul play is often detected by the assistants. This can be anything from a punch or a kick to a dangerous tackle. If one of the assistants spots any of theses infringements he will stick out his flag, horizontally in front of his body, to draw the attention of the referee. At the next stoppage the referee will consult with the assistant refree, and together they will decide whether any action needs to be taken.

The fourth official involved is a recent introduction to the team of law-enforcers. He is called the television match official, or TMO. He is in radio contact with the referee, but his duties are very limited at this stage. His assistance is only called upon for in-goal decisions. This means that the referee can only ask him to assist when the ball crosses either try-line. Often the ball is carried by a group of players, who then bundle over the line. The referee cannot always see whether the ball has been grounded, or if it has been actually held up off the ground by the defending team. Several cameras are set up on the try-lines, giving the TMO numerous angles to look at. He can advise the referee to award a try only if he can actually see whether the ball has been grounded. Even if it is clear that the ball seems to have been grounded but is out of sight, a try may not be awarded. He can also be asked to check whether a player may have stepped on or over the touch-line before scoring the try, which will result in a lineout to the opposition and not a try.

Players' positions and numbers

You will notice that the players all have numbers on their backs. These numbers indicate to us what every player's job is on the field. Each number corresponds with a position in the team. The numbers also help the referee if he has to identify a culprit or even address the player. You will often hear the referee say, "... Number 9 offside" or "Number 7—high tackle ..." and will see him pointing to whichever-numbered player is infringing. To maintain their impartiality, referees will always address players by their numbers, no matter how well they know their names.

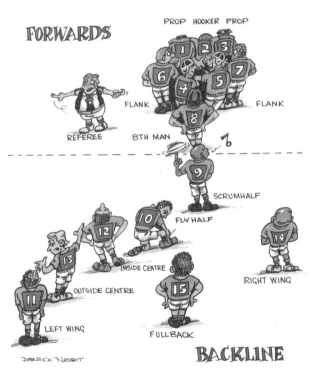

POSITIONS

FORWARDS

PROP HOOKER PROP

FLANK

FLANK

REFEREE

8TH MAN

SCRUMHALF

FLY HALF

INSIDE CENTRE

RIGHT WING

OUTSIDE CENTRE

LEFT WING

FULLBACK

DERRICK NESBIT

BACKLINE

There is no hard-and-fast rule that says a player *must* play in the position as indicated by the number on his back, but, more often than not, teams do tend to stick to it.

The illustration on the previous page indicates which numbers belong to which positions. I have arranged them in scrum formation so you know where each position slots in when they pack down. You will notice that numbers 1 to 8 are in a tighter bundle than numbers 9 to 15. They are often referred to as two separate units on the field. Numbers 1 to 8 are called 'forwards', while numbers 9 to 15 are called 'backs' or 'back-line' players. The forwards are generally physically bigger than the backs, because their jobs are of a more physical nature. The backs are usually fleeter of foot (and better-looking!) than the forwards. The better-looking bit is not a prerequisite, but is nevertheless often the case. (I hope no forwards read this; it may test my own fleetness of foot!) Here is a brief description of all the positions:

Numbers 1 and 3—Prop forwards

These are your power men. They are often the heaviest players on the field and are not known for their pace. They form the beacons of the scrum and their main duty is to ensure the scrums are stable and to secure a 'clean' ball to feed out to the waiting back-line. They are also called 'front-row men' or 'front rankers'.

Famous props: *Os du Randt, Johan Le Roux, Balie Swart, CJ van der Linde, Guthro Steenkamp, Tendai 'The Beast' Mtawarira*

Number 2—Hooker

The name describes them well—not because of their habits, but rather because of the fact that they are responsible for hooking the ball with their feet once it has been put into the scrum. They are also big guys, generally more agile than the props and as tough as nails. They have the added responsibility of throwing the ball into the lineout once it goes into touch. Together with the two props, these three are called the 'front row'.

Famous hookers: *John Smit, Uli Schmidt, Bismarck du Plessis, Sean Fitzpatrick, Keith Wood, Phil Kearns*

Numbers 4 and 5—Lock forwards

These will be the tallest guys on the park. They are easy to spot because they generally wear strapping around their heads. This is to protect their ears from the friction in the scrum. (Props have also been known to wear strapping around their heads, but nobody has really figured out why—it is theorized that they do this because they've seen the locks doing it, or because they don't want to hear Reffie screaming at them all day.) They are called locks because they 'lock' the scrum when they pack down behind the props and the hooker. Their main duty is to catch the ball when it is thrown into the lineouts, and hence the requirement for height. Together with the front row they have the very important duty of 'cleaning out' the defenders in the rucks to ensure a clean ball for the back-line. It is most often the locks who will catch the ball from kick-offs. They use their height to catch the ball above the heads of their opponents. The two locks and the front row form a unit referred to as the 'tight five' or 'tight forwards'.

Famous locks: *Victor Matfield, Bakkies Botha, Kobus Wiese, Frik du Preez, John Eales, Ian Jones, Louis Moolman*

Numbers 6 and 7—Flankers

Flanks get their name from the position where they pack down in the scrum. They bind on the side of the scrum onto the locks, behind the front row. They are medium-sized and agile players. Their duty is to scavenge the ball from the opposition and get to the breakdowns as soon as possible. If they can slow down the opposition ball or, better yet, steal it from them, it would be 'mission accomplished'. They also play an important role in the defensive strategy of the team, and tackling often defines these players.

Famous flankers: *Francois Pienaar, Corné Krige, Schalk Burger, Juan Smith, Richie McCaw, Ian MacDonald*

Number 8—Eighth-man

He packs down right at the back of the scrum and his role is very strategic. He often clears the ball from the scrum and links the forwards with the backs. He plays a very important defensive role and often falls back to field kicks and cover the back-line in defence. Traditionally they are tall guys, in order to provide an additional option in the lineouts. Together with the two flanks, numbers 6, 7 and 8 are also called 'loose forwards' or 'the back row'.

Famous eighth-men: *Bobby Skinstad, Pierre Spies, Ryan Kankowski, Joe van Niekerk, Tiaan Strauss, Morné du Plessis, Zinzan Brooke*

TIGHT 5   LOOSE TRIO

Number 9—Scrum-half

Most often this is the shortest guy on the field. Beware, though—he is well known for his high levels of 'attitude'. I have yet to meet two scrum-halves who actually like each other. They have a very important job on the field. The main duties include putting the ball into the scrum, clearing the ball from the set pieces and getting it to the back-line. Sniping breaks close to the fringes and tactical kicking complete the skill requirements of this little chipmunk. They are very nippy characters and, because they find themselves so close to the forwards, they are often required to make big tackles on the big guys. Being half their size, I suppose we can excuse the little bit of cockiness that goes with them.

Famous scrum-halves: *Joost van der Westhuizen, Fourie du Preez, George Gregan, Ricky Januarie, Gareth Edwards, John Robbie*

Number 10—Fly-half

He is the plan-maker, often referred to as 'the general'. Because he is the first receiver of the ball from the set pieces, he decides whether the ball gets kicked, passed or run with. The defence only starts approaching by the time he receives the ball, so he does have the most time to make these decisions. He needs to have the ability to kick the ball a long way and often takes responsibility for the goal-kicking. It is also his job to get the back-line moving, and he forms the pivot from which any attacks are launched. It is very important that these guys are good ball players; they can be compared to the quarter-back in American Football. Together with the scrum-half, they are called the half-backs.

It will be a close contest between fly-halves and wings as to which are the bigger posers! You will not often see fly-halves or wings wearing protective headgear; it may ruin their hairstyles. With a few exceptions, number 10s are not well known for their defence; in fact they can get out of the way with the stealth of a Mexican fence-climber rather than tackle somebody!

Famous fly-halves: *Naas Botha, André Pretorius, Hennie le Roux, Henry Honiball, Butch James, Daniel Carter, Johnny Wilkinson*

Numbers 12 and 13—Centres

The centres in the modern-day game have to be physically big, with enough ball skills and pace to create gaps and space for the outside backs. Their physical presence is important, as they often receive the ball with the defence very close—which means that they have no option other than making contact. It takes a great measure of physical strength to keep possession of the ball in these situations. Their weight also helps them to go forward in contact situations. They also need to be very strong on the defence. A tackle count after the game is usually a close race between the flanks and the centres, both positions making vast numbers of tackles in a match.

Famous centres: *Danie Gerber, Jean de Villiers, Jaque Fourie, Mannetjies Roux, Stirling Mortlock, Phillipe Sella, Dick Muir*

Numbers 11 and 14—Wings

Now here we have the glory boys. They are the fastest, strongest, smartest and sexiest players on the field (I'm not just saying it because I played there, of course)! Fancy footwork and strong defensive intuition are stock-standard requirements for these speedy individuals. The main job of the wings is to score the tries. The rest of the team battle away in order to put these guys into space. It doesn't help if you have a fat slow guy in space, does it? The wings are mostly the last receiver in the line, so if an overlap is created, they will be the person crossing the try-line. A wing with five metres or more space to work with is expected to beat the defence. A good wing is able to score the winning try, wink at a minimum of ten girls in the stand, and collect at least two phone numbers while on the field, with nobody being any the wiser

Famous wings: *James Small, Pieter Hendriks, David Campese, Bryan Habana, Carel du Plessis, Jonah Lomu, Lote Tuqiri, Ray Mordt*

Number 15—Full-back

No, he is not the fool at the back—he is the lonely fellow behind all the other players with the thankless job of fielding the ball that has been kicked by the opposition. He needs a high level of intuition and anticipation to ensure he positions himself in a place where he can catch the ball, should it be kicked. If the wings are not too busy fixing their hair, they can assist him with these duties. He needs to have the ability to kick the ball back if he gets isolated behind his own players, and also to run himself out of trouble if required. Goal-kicking is an important arrow in the full-back's quiver, and he is often called upon to use it. On attack, his job is to hide behind the ball-carriers and then explode into the line in an unexpected position, hopefully confusing the defence or breaking the line. Being tall (which they often are) helps them catch the ball above the heads of opposing players trying to contest the ball in the air.

Famous full-backs: *André Joubert, Francois Steyn, Gavin Johnson, Percy Montgomery, Thinus Delport, Serge Blanco, JPR Williams*

Numbers 16–22—Substitutes and Reserves

These are the guys on the bench who wait, with varying degrees of impatience, for their turn to play while the other 15 are on the field. Their numbers do not indicate any specific position. The seven players on the bench are generally made up as follows (this may differ from team to team, but it is compulsory to have an additional prop and a hooker on the bench. The reason for this is that very few people are strong and stupid enough to play in the front row, so you can't replace a front-row forward with any other player who is not trained in that position—the majority of us would probably die if we tried):

- 1 prop
- 1 hooker
- 1 lock
- 1 loose forward
- 1 scrum-half
- 2 utility backs (back-line players who can play in more than one position)

*****

I have often heard it said that rugby players are animals ... if that were the case, this is how they would probably pack down:

Props – *Rhinos*

Nothing to do with the size of the horn; just the short, stocky, powerful physique.

Hooker – *Lion*

He is strong, agile and as tough as a T-bone in Bangkok—fear is not an emotion he is familiar with.

Locks – *Giraffes*

Obviously for their height, and because they run funny.

Loose forwards – *Wolves or Hyenas*

They hunt and scavenge as a pack, and command fear as a unit.

Scrum-half – *Jackal*

Small but cunning, and very vocal.

Fly-half – *Owl*

Wise and calm, not very physical, plan-maker.

Centres – *Tigers*

Strong and gracious, with very few natural enemies.

Wings – *Cheetahs*

Pure pace, glory and hair!

Full-back – *Ostrich*

Fast and tall, with a hell of a kick.

Field positions and game plan

Game plans and strategies differ from game to game and depend on the opposition, the weather conditions and even the altitude. The only constant factor is that team strategies are based on where the players find themselves on the field.

When reference is made to a team's try-line, it refers to the try-line they are defending. The opponents' try-line is the one they are attacking. Any area before the halfway line belongs to one team; the other half belongs to the opponents.

An example of a very conservative game plan might be as follows:

Game plan A

1) From our own try-line-up to the 10-metre line in our half (red area) we will kick the ball as far as possible downfield and make them run at us from the back. Our defensive lines should rush up and force mistakes and attempt to trap them in their half.
2) From our 10-metre line-up to their 10-metre line we will use our forwards to drive the ball upfield; when we clear it to the backs they will crash it up and bring it back into the forwards, keeping it tight. The intention here is to engage as many defenders as possible while forward progress is being made (orange area).
3) From their 10-metre line-up (green area) we will spread the ball wide and try to get the ball to the wings and attack out wide. If we have sucked in enough defenders through the driving, there should be some space on the outside.

This is just one example of a basic plan, but it may well change within minutes. The score and game situation need to be assessed by the captain and adjustments made as required. Players also need to read the situation in front of them and be brave enough to deviate from the plan if they think it would benefit the team. If a player does this and his deviation from the plan does not work, he exposes himself to a great deal of slander and ridicule from his teammates and fans alike.

Rassie Erasmus, former coach of the Cheetahs and current director of rugby at Western Province, made headlines when he climbed up on the roof of the stadium with different-coloured lights and shone them down at the players. They had a strategy planned for each colour. As per the areas mentioned before (red, orange and green), the players would know what was expected of them when they saw which colour light the coach had turned on.

Reserves and substitutions
These are the seven players on the bench. They are there for two reasons:

Injury
If one of the 15 players on the park is injured and cannot continue playing, someone needs to take his place.

Substitution
In the modern-day game, coaches are allowed to substitute a player on the field with one of the players on the bench. The coach can do this for one of three reasons:

- It could be pre-planned. The coach would tell one player to play his heart out for 60 minutes and then bring on the fresh legs of a substitute. This often happens when a player returns from injury and is not yet 100% fit. It could also be the case with older players, where they are still good enough to compete at the highest level but cannot do so for 80 minutes.
- Tactical change. The coach may decide to change the game plan, which might require one or more of the specific strengths of the substitutes. For example, if the coach wanted to kick more and the player on the field does not have the kicking abilities of the substitute, the coach will make the substitution.
- Player loss of form. If one of the players keeps making mistakes or

seems to be off his game for whatever reason, the coach will make a substitution. This is harsh on the player because he does not have the opportunity to correct his mistakes, but that is the reality of the professional game.

The twist with the substitution law is that the coach cannot substitute a player and then bring the original player back on the field later. Once he has been substituted, his game is over, with two exceptions:

- The blood-bin. With the possibility of disease being transferred through blood, the referee must stop the game and ask any bleeding player to leave the field to get stitched up or somehow get the bleeding stopped. He can be substituted and will be allowed back on the field once the bleeding has stopped.
- If either of the props or the hooker has been substituted and his substitute in turn is injured, the referee will allow the original player back on the field. The reason for this is simply that a team cannot force a player from a different position to pack down in the front row as it will risk serious neck injury. If the substitute and the original player are injured, the referee is forced to have uncontested scrums. In this instance some other player will pack down in the prop's position, but nobody will push and they will basically just stand there in scrum formation and bind together to get the game started.

Sin-bin and shower
The worst way a referee can penalize a team is by giving one, or more, of their players a card. This can be either a yellow or a red card.

Yellow card
If a player receives a yellow card, it means he must leave the field

of play for a period of ten minutes. His team is not allowed to bring a substitute on, which means they must play with 14 men until the ten minutes are up. The offending player will sit on the side-line in a spot called the 'sin-bin'. Once back on the field, he is under serious scrutiny from the referee and a further yellow-card offence will automatically mean a red card.

Red card

If a player receives a red card, he can go and shower. His team will have to play with 14 men for the rest of the game, regardless of how long that may be.

Cards are dished out for two reasons:

Foul play

This is when a player takes physical aggression beyond the laws of the game. This could include a punch, a kick or even a dangerous tackle. Depending on the severity of the offence, the referee will decide whether to send him to the sin-bin for ten minutes, or off to the showers with a red card.

Professional foul

A professional foul is when a player deliberately infringes close to his own try-line, which results in the attacking team losing the ball, or being prohibited from scoring a try because of this infringement. An example of this is when a player deliberately goes offside to stop the opposition from scoring. Often when a ruck is formed close to the try-line, defending players interfere with the ball on the ground to slow down the attacking team's ball, which gives the defence more time to get organized. If a referee spots this, he may dish out a yellow card.

Summary

Four officials are involved in a rugby match:

- The referee
- Two assistant referees (formerly touch-judges)
- A television match official (TMO)

Player numbers and positions:
- 1 & 3—props
- 2—hooker
- 4 & 5—locks
- 6 & 7—flanks
- 8—eighth-man
- 9—scrum-half
- 10—fly-half
- 12 & 13—centres
- 11 & 14—wings
- 15—full-back
- 16–22—reserves and substitutions

The coach can substitute any of the players on the field with one of the substitutes at any time.

Once a player has been substituted, he is not allowed back on the field of play, with two exceptions:

- A blood-bin injury
- A front-row forward is required

- The harshest way to penalize a team is by giving one or more of their players a card. The card can be yellow or red.
- A yellow card means that the player must leave the field for a period of ten minutes. During these ten minutes, the team will play with 14 men.
- A red card means the player is sent off for the remainder of the game, regardless of how long that may be. The team will play with 14 men for the rest of the game.
- Red or yellow cards are dished out for foul play or professional fouls.

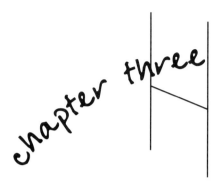

Let the game begin!

The game of rugby has much in common with relationships. The moment the game starts, both teams are bound by a set of rules. Once a player deviates from these rules, proceedings come to a temporary halt. The way in which the game restarts is determined by the level of menace, deceit and recklessness involved in the infringement. Sometimes the restart contains a measure of punishment; at other times it is simply a way to get things going after a quiet patch.

The biggest difference exists in the form of a referee. He decides when the rules have been broken; he also decides which measure of punishment is required and applies it equally to both teams. No wonder men are so crazy about rugby. It is simple and it makes sense— which is not always the case in relationships!

Every relationship has its little elves. Elves are those things that cause trouble in a relationship which can lead to an adjustment of the rules. Those naughty little elves also rear their heads in rugby. The rugby bosses decided to adjust a number of the laws during the 2008 season and called it the ELVs or 'Experimental Law Variations'. The word 'experimental' is in the name because these new laws are being implemented until August 2009. After that, the powers-that-be will decide which of the ELVs will become a permanent fixture in the law books and which ones will be scrapped. Appendix 1 contains a summary of all the ELVs.

The toss
Just before the game starts, the referee meets with the two captains. A coin is tossed to determine which team will kick off, and in which direction the teams will play

The four aspects of rugby
The game can be divided into four main categories:

- Kick-offs
- Set pieces
- Ball in play
- Punishment measures

Every time the whistle goes, the game will stop and one of the above restart mechanisms will be implemented, outlined as follows:

The kick-off

Kick-off from the halfway line
This is how the game begins. The kick-off is taken from the centre spot of the field; the kicking team will start proceedings with a drop kick into the opponents' half of the field. Every time points are scored, the game will restart with this kick-off. The team which conceded the points will take the kick-off. After half-time, the game will also restart with a kick-off from the halfway line. The team that kicked off at the beginning of the game will now receive.

This kick-off has to travel at least ten metres before the players from the kicking team can touch it or it goes into touch. If the kick is short, the receivers can catch it and play, but then the referee will let play continue and any other advantage would be lost. The broken 10-metre line is there to show the referee whether the ball has travelled ten metres, and it also gives the kicker a target to aim at.

The 22-metre kick-off

There is one other kick-off in the game of rugby. It is called the 22-metre kick-off. Taken as a drop kick from either side's 22-metre line, it is used to restart the game when the ball has rolled over the dead-ball line behind the posts or the ball has been grounded behind the try-line by the defending team, as long as they did not carry it over the line themselves. If this is the case, a scrum restart will be awarded to their opponents five metres from the try-line. This kick does not have to travel ten metres; it is legal as long as it crosses the 22-metre line.

Set pieces

The lineout

The lineout is how the game gets restarted when the ball—or a player carrying the ball—goes over the touch-line. Unlike in tennis, on the line is *out*. This is when the forwards from both sides stand in a straight line behind each other, one metre from their opponents, and one of the hookers throws the ball into the middle of these two lines. The players will then jump in the air and attempt to catch it. There is a distinct advantage to the team throwing the ball in, as they will have a prearranged code with the thrower, telling him where to throw it, and they will have practised the timing of the jump. The opponents can merely guess and try to steal the ball by catching it from the throw or deflecting it to their side. The last team to have touched the ball prior to it going into touch will concede the throw-in. There is one exception—kicks from a penalty. If a team kicks the ball out from a penalty, they will also throw the ball into the lineout, making this a very attractive attacking option.

Short lineout

The laws do not dictate that all eight forwards have to be in the lineout. The team that throws the ball in determines how many players will be committed to the line. Their opponents will generally use the same number of players to contest for the ball—but, in terms of the ELVs, this is not compulsory. All the forwards who are not part of the lineout have to retreat ten metres unless they use one of them as a the scrum-half. One player is allowed to stand in that 10-metre area, because he has to distribute the ball from the lineout to the other players who are ten metres back.

The quick throw

If a player catches the ball outside the field of play, he can execute a quick throw by passing the ball in-field to one of his teammates, or throw it up in the air and catch it himself and play from there. The following rules will apply in this instance:

A quickie can be exciting … but it's sometimes a dangerous thing to attempt.

- The player throwing the ball in must be outside the field of play when he throws it in.
- The ball must travel over the five-metre line before being caught by a teammate or by the player himself.
- The throw can only be taken on or behind the point where the ball went out.
- A quick throw has to be taken with the same ball that was kicked out, and it may not have been touched by any other person (a reserve, assistant referee, spectator, ball boy, medical personnel or streaker, for that matter.) If the ball *did* touch any other person, the quick throw will not be allowed and the referee will call them back to form a lineout on the spot where the ball crossed the touch-line.

Kicking the ball into touch
The ball can only be kicked directly into touch (without bouncing in

the field of play) if the kicking player is kicking the ball from inside his own 22-metre area. If he kicks it directly into touch from outside his 22-metre area, the lineout will be held in line with the spot he kicked the ball from.

In terms of the new laws, a player may only kick the ball directly into touch if he gathered the ball inside his 22-metre area, and kicks it from there. This means he can't kick it directly into touch if his teammate passed him the ball from outside the 22-metre area, or if he caught the ball outside and then ran back in. Doing this will result in a lineout in line with the spot where he kicked the ball from, putting his team under huge pressure.

The exception to this rule is, once again, the penalty. If a team elects to kick the ball out from a penalty, it may go directly into touch, regardless of where they are on the field, and they will have the throw into the lineout.

The scrummage
Scrums are awarded to the opponents for minor infringements with no menace involved. Conceding a scrum does contain an element of punishment, in that the infringing team surrenders control.

This is the part of the game where the referee gives instructions sounding like the choreography of a porn movie:

Crouch! Touch! Pause! Engage!

It is the true physical confrontation of the match, where the big guys get to prove their worth. In a scrum, all eight forwards of the one team scrum down against the eight forwards of their opponents. They huff and puff and squeeze each other with a fury that makes demons shudder. The referee will award the scrum to a particular team by blowing his whistle and pointing his arm in the direction of the team who has won the scrum feed. That team's scrum-half gets to feed the ball into the scrum and, most often, that team will win the ball. If the defending team wins the ball from a scrum, it is called a 'tight head' or a 'heel against the head'.

The two props, numbers 1 and 3, have different specialities, and are called alternately a 'loose-head prop' or a 'tight-head prop'. Number 1 is always the loose-head and number 3 the tight-head. The reasons for the names are simple—they are the pillars of the scrum, and the way that they pack down against the front row of the other team gives them their names as illustrated below.

The scrum-half will always feed the scrum on his team's loose-head side. The defending team will receive the ball from their tight-head side. Hence the name 'tight-head' when a team wins a scrum off the other team's feed. This is somewhat rare but it does happen often enough to need a name.

The scrum is a good attacking platform for the backs, because the loose forwards have to stay bound to the scrum until the ball is cleared. If they break away before the ball is out of the scrum, a penalty will be awarded against them. Because they have to stay bound, it gives the backs some room to work with before those flanks come along to make tackles.

The defending back-line has to stay five metres behind the eighth-man's feet while the ball is in the scrum. If the scrum wheels, they still have to stay five metres behind the feet of the last player bound to the scrum. This is the invisible offside line. If they creep up beyond that line, the referee will award a penalty to the attacking team.

They are allowed to breach that line the moment the ball is cleared from the scrum.

Many strategies and tactics exist at scrum time, because one team will often realize that they do not have the power to take their opponents on with brute force alone, and that wheeling the scrum or clearing the ball very fast would serve them better. If the defending team manages to wheel the scrum through 180 degrees, the referee will blow his whistle and award a new scrum to the successful swingers.

The ball in play

Once the ball emerges from the scrum or lineout, the ball-carrier may run into a contact situation which can result in either a ruck or a maul.

The tackle situation

If the ball-carrier is tackled and brought to ground in the tackle, he has one second to place the ball so that his teammates can come and help him secure possession. Once that second is over, he must release it. If he fails to do so, the referee will award a free kick to the other side.

The tackler is obliged to roll away from the ball if he is obstructing the efforts of the tackled player's teammates to get to the ball. If he does not roll away, or at least make an effort to do so, the referee will award a free kick to the attacking side.

If the tackler can get to his feet, he is allowed to lean over and pick up the ball that the tackled player has placed (remember, he is *not* allowed to hold onto it on the ground). The next player, from either side, who arrives is also allowed to pick the ball up, as long as he is on his feet while doing so.

What is a ruck

As soon as there are three or more players involved in this tackle situation on the ground, it is called a ruck—that heap of players on the ground, fighting to win the ball for their team with other players diving on top of them like men possessed. The teammates of the tackled player have the duty to clean any defenders within a one-metre radius of the ball by pushing and bouncing them out the way. As soon as the ruck is formed, nobody is allowed to grab the ball with their hands. You will often hear the referee shouting "Ruck!" or "Hands out!", which tells the players that they are not allowed to try and pick up the ball with their hands. This was done to improve the flow of the game, because if everybody is fighting for the ball on the ground with their hands, it will rarely ever emerge. The scrum-half is allowed to dig for the ball with his hands as long as his intention is to clear the ball from the ruck—Reffie will know!

Players who join the ruck are not allowed to come in from the side of the heap or from the opponent's side. They have to come in from behind and through the 'gate', which is formed by the head and feet of the teammate on the ground.

The feet of the last man involved in the ruck is the offside line. Any player who is not a part of the ruck has to stay behind these feet. Should he creep up past that line, he will be penalized.

What is a maul?

This is a bundle of players, caked around the ball, while everybody is still on their feet, almost like the strip show at a bachelor party. The maul is used as an attacking strategy, where one player will carry the ball and the others will pack around him and power their way forward. The laws did not allow the defenders to collapse the maul, but the ELVs say they may! This strategy is often used from an attacking lineout close to the opponents' try-line.

Punishment measures

The free kick

The free kick is awarded for offences that contain an element of malice but do not have serious consequences. This is when Barry is a bit over-friendly with the girl wearing the least clothing at the party. The more beers he has, the more often he is spotted in her company. He does not necessarily concede points, but you seriously want to give him a 'free kick' in exactly that area of his anatomy which is reminding him of the 'slutty' presence.

The experimental laws introduced in 2008 made the free kick a frequently-used method of punishment. Many infringements which were punished by penalties and scrums in the past, have now been amended to free kicks.

Reffie will award a free kick by raising his arm, bent at the elbow, in the direction of the non-offending team. This means the offending team immediately has to retreat ten metres. The team awarded the free kick has four basic options:

- They can decide to kick the ball downfield towards the touch-line, or any other form of kick with no pressure, because the defenders are ten metres away. They may not kick the ball directly into touch, unless they are in their 22-metre area.

- They can take a 'quick tap', which means any player (normally the scrum-half) can tap the ball with his foot and then start an attacking movement by running at the defence or passing the ball to another player to do so. If the defenders have not retreated ten metres, they are not allowed to touch him until he has run at least five metres. If they tackle him before the five-metre run, the referee can award another free kick, this time ten metres *closer* to the defenders' try-line.

- The attacking team will only be allowed one quick tap. Once another ten metres has been given, the attacking team must wait until the defence has retreated the ten metres before commencing play.

- A pre-planned move. The defence is ten metres away, which gives the attacking team space to execute a rehearsed move with 'dummy runners' trying to create some confusion, and the ball-carrier running into space.

- The attacking captain can elect to have a scrum, rather than taking the free kick. Captains often do this if they have a dominant forward pack, and it also draws the defenders in if they want to spread the ball.

The penalty

A penalty is awarded for serious offences. These offences often include a healthy dose of malice and/or recklessness. The referee will award a penalty by blowing his whistle and putting one arm straight up in the air. He will turn in the direction of the team which is being awarded the penalty.

The team which has won the penalty has four basic options:

- Kick for goal: the kicker of the team can take a shot at goal. If he is successful, three points will be added to his team's tally.
- If it is too far to kick for goal, or the captain feels confident that his team can score a try from a lineout close to their opponents' line, they can kick for touch. Because it is a penalty, they will also have the throw into the lineout.
- They can also take a quick tap or execute a rehearsed move where the same rules will apply as for a free kick.
- The captain can also elect to have a scrum if he thinks this offers

his team better options. This will often be the case where a team is trailing by more than three points and time is almost up.

Yellow and red cards as punishment measures

Some offences are so blatant or reckless that a penalty alone is not enough punishment for the infringement. In this instance, Reffie will dish out a yellow or a red card, which means the perpetrator must leave the field.

Yellow card

If a player receives a yellow card, he has to leave the field for ten minutes and his team will have to play with 14 men for that period. The previous generation of rugby players called this 'the cooler', because players were sent there to 'cool off' a bit, usually after a fist-fight. Nowadays there are many other infringements which can land a player in the cooler (*see* Chapter 2).

Red card

This is the worst measure of punishment available to the referee—almost like the death penalty. Once a red card is given to a player, his team will have to make do without him for the rest of the match, and they are not allowed to bring a substitute on in his place. Needless to say, this puts the rest of the team under tremendous pressure and the red-carded individual is about as popular as a dose of clap. The play will restart through a penalty to the opposition.

Summary

- The game starts with the toss of a coin, where the captains meet to decide which side of the field they will defend and who will kick off.

- The game can be divided into four main categories:

  - kick-offs
  - set pieces

- ball in play
- measures of punishment

- There are two types of kick-offs:

  - the halfway line kick-off
  - the 22-metre line kick-off

- There are two types of set pieces:

  - the lineout
  - the scrummage

- Elements of the 'ball in play' scenario:

  - the tackle situation
  - the ruck
  - the maul

- Measures of punishment:

  - the free kick
  - the penalty
  - the yellow card
  - the red card

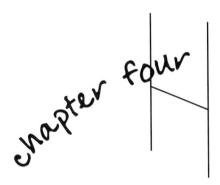

Why did that man blow the whistle?

Strangely, this is something that surprises most men, on the field or off. Even when the mistake is obvious, their faces will always be masks of complete amazement and perplexity. How is this possible?

Whatever the case may be, when the whistle goes, you have to stop doing what you were doing, and one of the restart methods will be implemented.

The advantage rule

When the referee spots an infringement, he will shout "Advantage!" and stick his arm out in the direction of the team that has the advantage. This tells the players that he is aware of a mistake, but he lets play go on to see whether the non-offending team can gain any advantage from the other team's mistake. It is up to the referee to decide whether sufficient advantage is gained and, if he feels it is, he will shout "Advantage over!" Play will then continue and that particular mistake is forgotten. If no advantage is gained, he will award the applicable restart on the spot where the offence occurred.

In the situation above, play will continue, as long as Barry is telling his new, scantily-clad friend how wonderful Sandy is and how madly in love he is with her. If he seems to have forgotten her in his conversation, play will be stopped and a free kick is probably in the offing.

Important note

For the puritans out there, it is not the intention of this chapter to outline the rule book in every technical detail. Only the main reasons for the whistle going will be listed, so that anyone will be able to follow the game easily. Even the experts among us are confused by 20 per cent of the decisions referees make—so as long as the layman understands the rules listed below, he or she will not be embarrassed watching a match.

A kick-off happens when ...

- The game is started by a kick-off from the halfway line in the middle of the field.
- To restart the game after half-time, the team which received the kick-off in the first half will take the kick from the middle of the field to get things going again.
- If any points are scored, the team which conceded the points will restart the game by a kick-off from the halfway line.

A 22-metre kick-off happens when ...

- The ball, or a player carrying the ball crosses the dead-ball line or the touch-lines behind the try-line (touch in goal).
- A player from the defending side dots the ball down behind his own try-line. (The 22-metre kick-off will only be awarded if he, or one of his teammates, did *not* carry the ball over their try-line.)

A scrum is awarded for ...

A knock-on or forward pass
If the ball goes forward from a player's hands—whether he passes it forward, drops it or fumbles a catch—a scrum will be awarded to the opponents.

Players being in front of the kicker at kick-off
Players chasing a kick-off have to be behind the kicker at the moment he strikes the ball.

The kick-off kick did not go ten metres
The kick-off from the halfway line needs to travel ten metres before it is played by the kicking team. If the ball does not go the distance a scrum will be awarded to the receiving team on the centre spot (a 22-metre kick only needs to cross the 22-metre line; there is no 10-metre rule for this kick-off).

Skew throw into the lineout
The hooker needs to throw the ball into the middle of the lineout—a skew throw will result in a scrum or a lineout to the opponents.

Ball not grounded, or it is inconclusive whether the ball was grounded in attempt to score a try
This often happens when the players maul the ball over the try-line. The defenders manage to keep the ball off the ground; or the referee (in conjunction with the TMO) cannot be certain that the ball was grounded. A scrum will be awarded to the attackers five metres from the line.

Accidental offside
If the ball-carrier accidentally runs into one of his own players in front of him, preventing the defence from getting to him, a scrum will be awarded against him. If it is done deliberately, a penalty will be awarded.

A lineout is awarded when …
- The ball goes into touch.
- The player carrying the ball goes into touch, or steps on the touch-line.
- The ball is kicked out on the full from a kick-off; the receiving captain will have the option of a lineout or a scrum.
- A skew throw into the lineout will also result in the defending captain choosing between a lineout throw or a scrum.

Where will the lineout be awarded?

- The lineout will be held at the point where the assistant referee determines the ball to have crossed the touch-line, *with one exception*—a kick from outside the 22-metre area. Should a player kick the ball directly into touch (without it bouncing in the field of play), the lineout will be held in line with the spot where he kicked it from.

- If a player kicks the ball from inside his own 22-metre area, he may kick the ball directly into touch, as long as he caught the ball in the 22-metre area, or the set piece prior to the kick was already in the 22-metre area. He may not kick it directly into touch if a teammate received the ball outside the 22-metre and then passed it to him inside the 22-metre area. In this instance, the lineout will be held in line with the spot where he kicked the ball from.

- If the ball is kicked while the kicker is outside of his 22-metre area, the ball needs to bounce, be caught or at least be touched by a player inside the field of play before going into touch.

A free kick is awarded when ...

From a scrum

Premature engaging

You will recall that the referee gives the instructions "*Crouch! Touch! Pause! Engage!*" If one team engages prematurely, not only is it highly disappointing, but will also result in a free kick being awarded to the opponents.

Skew feed

If the scrum-half feeds the ball under his own hooker's feet, a free kick can be awarded against him.

From a lineout

'Bokking' or dummy-throwing
If the hooker has a dummy throw, or feints, a free kick will awarded against him.

Taking too long
If the team takes too long to throw the ball into the lineout, a free kick can be given against them.

Closing the gap
The one-metre gap between the two lines must be maintained until the ball leaves the hooker's hands from the throw. If one team closes this gap prior to the ball being thrown, a free kick will be awarded against that team.

From a ruck
This must be the hardest area to referee, and hence the majority of free kicks are awarded as a result of a ruck infringement. There are so many things to look for and it all happens in a split-second. Poor Reffie! These are the commonest causes of free kicks:

Tackler not rolling away
The tackler must roll away and allow the ball-carrier to place the ball and give his teammates access to it.

Hands in the ruck
Once a ruck is formed, no hands are allowed on the ball.

Holding on
A tackled player has one second to place the ball. Thereafter, he must release it. If he holds onto it so that the opposition cannot take it from him, he will be penalized.

Tackled ball

If a player has been tackled but, because of the way he fell and the other players piling in, it is unlikely that the ball will emerge from the ruck, the referee will award a free kick to the defending team.

Static maul—use it or lose it

If a maul becomes static, the referee will shout out "Use it!" once. This gives the attacking team the opportunity to clear the ball or get the maul moving again. If they get it moving forward again they will have to clear it if it becomes static again. If they fail to do so, a free kick will be awarded to the defence.

From a kick

Catching a mark

If a kick is caught inside a player's own 22-metre area and he shouts "Mark!" as he catches the ball, the referee will award a free kick to that team. The challenge is to scream loud enough for the referee to hear the catcher above the noise of the crowd. In this instance, whichever player caught the 'mark' is the player who must take the tap, or kick, or whatever course of play he decides.

A penalty is awarded when ...

From a scrum

Illegal scrummaging or binding

This can get rather technical, but suffice it to say that the props have to bind onto each other in a specific way and are not allowed to collapse or 'wheel' the scrum deliberately. They are also not allowed to lift their opponents off the ground.

Loose-forward binding

The flanks and the eighth-man have to remain bound to the scrum until the ball emerges. If they break away before the ball is out, they will concede a penalty.

Hands in the scrum

Once the ball is fed into the scrum, it may only be hooked out with the players' feet. Anybody who puts a naughty hand on the ball will be penalized.

Offside

The back-line needs to stay five metres behind the scrum. For the scrum-half, the offside line is the ball—so, as the ball is fed into the scrum and hooked towards the back, the defending scrum-half can follow his opponent, as long as he stays behind the ball. If he decides not to follow his opponent but rather to chase the fly-half, he is not allowed to move more than one metre away from the scrum. If he does, the ELVs say it is fine, but he has to fall five metres back, just like the rest of the back-line.

From a lineout

Pulling down

If a player jumps to catch the ball, his opponents are not allowed to interfere with him. They may attack the ball, but they can't prevent him from jumping or pull him down, even if he has caught the ball.

Offside

Both back-lines must be ten metres away from the lineout. The scrum-half is the only player allowed in that 10-metre area, and it does not have to be the actual scrum-half; it can be any player as long as there is only one. The lineout will be deemed to be over once the forwards have caught the ball and the maul has moved out of the 'box' created by the two lines. The back-line will then be allowed to creep up and the feet of the last man in the ruck/maul will constitute the new offside line.

From the ruck and maul

Unnecessary raking
You can only rake the ball with your boots—not an opposing player's kidney. If the raking is not on the ball, the referee will penalize the raking player.

Coming in from the side
Players joining the ruck must come from behind the last man's feet and through the gate—they cannot dive in from the side.

Going off feet

Even if players come into the ruck from behind, they are not allowed to dive in and deliberately go off their feet to secure or win the ball.

Offside

The last man's feet in the ruck is the offside line for players not involved in the ruck. They have to stay behind until the ball is out. A well-known term in rugby is 'the ball is only out when a bird can shit on it'. The reality is that players often think

the bird will be able to get to the ball when only a small portion of it is in sunlight. These birds are not B-52 bombers with precision target-seeking turds—the *entire* ball must be out before the defenders can advance!

From kicks

Players in front of the kicker

If one player kicks the ball, his teammates may not chase it if they were in front of him when he kicked it. They can only start advancing when the kicker himself, or a teammate who was behind him, has run past them.

10-metre radius

If a kick comes down and teammates of the kicker are in the vicinity of the spot where the ball is coming down, they have to retreat and move at least ten metres away from where the ball comes down, otherwise they will be offside. If the ball is partially charged down or has been touched by an opposing player when it is kicked, everybody is automatically onside and they will not have to retreat or wait for a player behind the kicker to put them onside.

Tackling a player in the air

Defenders fielding a kick will often jump into the air in order to catch the ball above the heads of opponents who are competing for the ball. You are not allowed to tackle a player until his feet are on the ground. If you tackle him while he is in the air, a penalty will be awarded and you risk being sent to the sin-bin.

From general play

High tackle

Any tackle above the shoulders is a high tackle and will be penalized.

Spear tackle
This is when a tackle is made and the defender picks up the legs of his opponent, flips him over and drives his head into the ground. This very often results in a yellow or even a red card.

Tackling without using arms
Shoulder-charging is not allowed. You *must* use your arms in a tackle.

Obstruction
This happens if the ball is passed to a player who is running behind his teammates who, in turn, are obstructing the defence from getting to the ball-carrier.

Dissent
Basically this means you can't swear at the referee, say anything about his sister or his mother or any other family member.

Diving on a player on the ground
If a player is on the ground you can try to rip the ball from him, but you can't go off your feet and dive on him. The ex-All Black eighth-man, Murray Mexted (who is a commentator today) described this

rule best in one of his commentaries: "I think this rule is hard to apply because the moment you see a man on the ground the first thing you want to do is go down on him." If you say so, Murray …

Foul play
This can be anything from punching, kicking scratching, biting or any other soccer-spectator-like behaviour. If done blatantly, it can earn you a yellow or red card.

Summary
- The sound of the whistle blowing will indicate the start of the game and stop proceedings whenever a mistake is made.

- The game is started by a kick-off from the halfway line in the middle of the field at the beginning of the game, as well as after half-time.

- A 22-metre kick-off is taken if the ball goes over the dead-ball line, or if a player dots the ball down behind his own line.

- A scrum is awarded for less serious offences. The most common reasons for a scrum are:
  - a knock-on or forward pass
  - kick-off not going ten metres
  - players in front of the kicker at kick-off
  - skew throw into the lineout
  - ball not grounded, or inconclusive whether the ball was grounded in an attempt to score a try
  - accidental offside
  - a captain choosing a scrum rather than a free kick

- A lineout is awarded when the ball goes into touch, or the player carrying the ball steps on the line or into touch.
- On the line means out!

- Free kicks are awarded for offences more serious than a scrum restart but not as serious as a penalty offence. The most common reasons for free kicks are:
  - tackler not rolling away
  - holding on to the ball on the ground
  - hands in the ruck
  - coming in from the side of the ruck or maul
  - premature engaging into the scrum
  - feeding the ball under the hooker's feet
  - dummy throw into the lineout
  - taking too long to throw the ball into the lineout
  - closing the gap in the lineout
  - calling a mark

- Penalties are awarded for the worst offences. The most common causes for penalties are:
  - illegal scrummaging
  - hands in the scrum
  - offside at set pieces, as well as rucks and mauls (in most instances, the last man's feet represent the offside line)
  - interfering with an opposing jumper in the lineout
  - unnecessary raking
  - going off your feet at the ruck
  - being in front of the advancing kicker before being put onside
  - not retreating from the 10-metre radius of the ball if in front of the kicker
  - tackling a player in the air
  - high tackle
  - shoulder tackle
  - spear tackle
  - obstruction
  - dissent
  - diving on a player on the ground
  - foul play

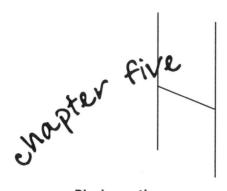

Playing options

Prior to running out onto the park, every team will have a plan and a strategy for what they are going to do in certain areas on the field. The challenge for players is that the situation on the field may allow, or even encourage, a course of action different to what the game plan requires. The top players are able to deviate from predetermined plans by reading the situation in front of them and, in so doing, produce a better result than the plan would have given them. It is this ability that sets them apart from other players.

Every time a player receives the ball he has split-seconds to make a decision about how he is going to play. He has three basic options:

- he can kick the ball
- he can run with the ball
- he can pass the ball to a teammate

As spectators, it is not always clear to us why players take a particular course of action, mainly because the execution of what they wanted to achieve was not good enough, or because the defence did something they did not anticipate. There are, however, a few basic rules that players generally stick to—but even the most professional players do some inexplicable things on the field that baffle the best rugby brains around. So don't despair if someone does something that just doesn't make sense—it happens all the time.

Following are the most common answers to some of the most frequently-asked questions:

Why did he kick?
This is a question I often ask, because I think we see far too much aimless kicking going on. If kicks don't go where they are intended, the kicker has achieved nothing other than giving the ball to the opponents. Having said this, a clever kicking game has won many a match and it definitely has its place.

There are three types of kicks:

- the defensive kick
- the attacking kick
- the scoring kick

The defensive kick
If a team is in their own 22-metre area, they are close to their try-line. It is a high-risk area. If they choose to run with the ball in this area, they risk dropping it or making some other mistake that would give possession to their opponents, which could clearly be detrimental so close to their try-line. They also risk conceding a penalty, which means that the opposing team could easily score points by kicking for goal. Generally, teams do not want to mess around in this area, and if they win the ball they will kick it as far as possible away from their try-line and into touch. The drawback here is that the opponents will have the throw-in at the lineout, but at least it gives your team's defence time to reorganize and gets you further away from your try-line.

In their own 22-metre area, players can kick the ball directly into touch. This is a safe option, because you can get the ball off the park and hence enforce a lineout restart where your defence can be organized and you put some distance between your try-line and the attackers. Kickers who can kick the ball a long way are very valuable in this situation. In short, this type of kick is used to improve field position.

Often a player will catch the ball behind all his teammates and, with attackers chasing him down, it is wise for him to kick the ball back to the opponents, as opposed to becoming isolated and caught in possession behind his teammates. If he catches the ball outside his own 22-metre area, he cannot kick the ball directly into touch, which means he also risks one of the opponents catching the ball in the field of play and launching a counter-attack. If he does kick it out on the full, the opponents will be awarded a lineout in line with the spot where he kicked the ball from and not where it went out.

The attacking kick

An attacking kick is a kick that is rarely intended to go out, unless its destination is five metres or less from the opposing try-line. Some captains also prefer kicking the ball out close to the opposing try-line from a penalty, as opposed to kicking for goal. This will mean they get a lineout throw close to the opposing try-line, and a very good chance of mauling it over the line for a try. The difficulty in the decision is to opt for a guaranteed three points from a goal-kick,

or a riskier, possible seven points from scoring a try. Many captains have endured cartloads of criticism for making the wrong decision in this situation. The game situation will dictate what the captain will decide. It

will depend what the score is, how much time is left in the game, the reliability of the goal-kicker and, of course, the maturity of the captain. I have seen many teams lose a game because the captain thinks like a cowboy instead of making the correct basic rugby decisions. Of course the 'wrong' decisions often bear fruit for captains and then we love those cowboy decisions.

Another attacking kick is the called the 'up and under', or 'Gary Owen'. It got its name from a club in Limerick, Ireland, called Gary Owen. This team used the high kick as an attacking strategy so often that people started calling the kick a 'Gary Owen'. This is a high kick, intended to put pressure on the catcher because he has to wait for the ball to come down, knowing that opposing players are rushing towards him at full speed. A perfect up-and-under is just far enough to ensure that the chaser gets to the spot where the ball comes down, at full pace. The attacking team can often regain possession from such a kick by catching it above the heads of the defenders, or by forcing the defenders' catcher to drop the ball by contesting for it in the air, or tackling him as he catches it and ripping it away from him.

The grubber kick or rolling kick is another way of placing your opponents under pressure. This is often effective because the odd-shaped rugby ball does not bounce predictably. This means the defenders have to turn around to chase it down and it may not bounce kindly for them. The grubber kick is often used where the ball is kicked over the opposing try-line for the speedsters to chase. If they can outrun the defenders and beat them to the ball, they simply have to fall on it to score a try. This is very difficult to defend against because there are not enough players to tackle on the front line and cover behind every defender. For the attacking team it is still a risky thing to do because if the ball goes over the dead-ball line, the defenders will be awarded a scrum from where the ball was kicked. If the defenders get to the ball before the chasers, they can dot it down and a 22-metre kick-off will be awarded, which means the excellent field position has been wasted. These kicks need to be very well executed because if the ball goes too far, too close or too wide, possession of the ball is given back to the opponents.

Scoring kicks

The three types of scoring kicks have already been described. To summarize, they are:

- the penalty kick   3 points
- the drop kick   3 points
- the conversion kick   2 points

Why did he run?

This is always exciting to watch and really the reason for the spectators being there—but in certain instances it can be very dangerous and cost the team dearly. In the opposing 22-metre area it goes without saying that launching a running attack is the way to go, but in your *own* 22-metre area it could be suicide. If you get isolated close to your own try-line, you almost certainly guarantee points to the opposition. However, if you manage to break through from your own try-line and find enough support to score a try, you will undoubtedly be the hero of the day and become an instant crowd favorite. Once again, making the correct decisions in such circumstances differentiates great players from the merely mediocre. Bear in mind that the view on the field from the players' perspective is very different to the view we have on television, or even from the

stands. The decision to run with the ball is generally made when the player sees some space in front of him, or realizes that his teammates next to him are not in better positions than he is, even if it means running into a wall of defenders.

RISKY MOVE - WORKING FAMOUSLY

The conservative, and most often correct, thing to do close to your own try-line is to kick the ball as far as possible into touch and thereby force a lineout restart. Your defending teammates will be expecting this, however, which can create some laziness in their follow-up. This could be a great opportunity for the attacking team to run into space, using the element of surprise and catching the defence off guard. Good players are able to identify when the time is right to run from the deep, but even the best have been caught behind their teammates. This creates huge pressure for the team and usually some verbal abuse from the bigger guys—but the flipside of the coin is guaranteed hero-worship from supporters should you succeed. A hard decision to make, but that's rugby!

The core reason a player will hold onto the ball is when he thinks he has a chance to break the defence. Be it by running into space or through a wall of defenders using his strength, the end goal remains the same.

Why did he pass?

The obvious answer to this question is that one of his teammates was in a better position than he was to execute the kick or running attack intended. Sometimes a player will pass the ball because his teammate is better able to execute whatever move is called for. An example of this is when a player catches the ball and the team kicker is next to him. If kicking is what needs to be done, it is wise to give the specialist kicker the ball. In turn, the specialist kickers are most often not the biggest guys. If there is no time to kick, he would be wise to pass the ball to one of his forwards who is better able to deal with the inevitable physical confrontation.

Players also pass the ball when it is part of a rehearsed move. It is here were we often see a player passing the ball to a teammate who has three defenders on top of him, and flattens him as he receives the ball. This is where the better players will realize that the rehearsed move is not on, and either hold on to the ball or pass it to a different player who is in a better position.

In short, passing the ball should lead to a teammate with more time and space to do what needs to be done.

Summary
- The ball-carrier has three basic playing options:

  - he can kick the ball
  - he can run with the ball
  - he can pass the ball

- There are three types of kicks:

  - the defensive kick
  - the attacking kick
  - the scoring kick

- A player will run with the ball if he is in space and he thinks has a chance to break the defensive line.

- A player will pass the ball to a teammate if his teammate is in a better position, or has a better ability to do the specific job that needs to be done at that moment.

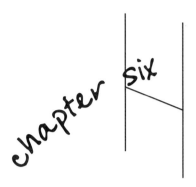

Teams and competitions

In order to hold your own in a rugby conversation in the coffee area at work, you will need to know who's who in the zoo. It really is a zoo, with every team nowadays calling themselves some sort of animal. From their names it is not always obvious where they are from and whom they represent. You thought it was simple because all men are just pigs … although when playing rugby they are often transformed into more elegant creatures, even if only by name. Before you are introduced to all the different teams in South Africa, it is important to understand how tournaments are won and lost.

How a tournament works

Points are recorded on a tournament log and the team with the most points on the log wins the competition, **or** the top four teams on the log play semi-finals and the winners of those games battle it out for the championship, depending on the specific tournament rules.

How does the log work?

An example what a tournament log looks like, as well as what all the abbreviations stand for, is illustrated as follows:

Team	P	W	D	L	F	A	B	P
A	2	2	0	0	80	20	2	10
B	2	1	0	1	50	40	1	5
C	2	0	0	2	20	60	0	0

The abbreviations mean the following:

P	=	games played
W	=	games won
D	=	games drawn
L	=	games lost
F	=	total number of points scored (For)
A	=	total number of points conceded (Against)
B	=	bonus points
P	=	log points

The log points in the last column are what determines who wins the competition or who gets to play in the semi-finals. Some logs also have a PD column. This stands for 'points difference' and is simply the difference between the 'points for' and 'points against'. The 'points for' and 'points against' are also shown on the log because if two teams end up with the same number of log points, the team with the bigger positive-points difference will be ranked above the other.

How do teams accumulate points on the log?

Every competition will dictate in its rules what system it will use to accumulate points on the log. The majority of tournaments will use one of the two systems illustrated as follows:

4–2–1 system
- 4 points for a win
- 2 points for a draw
- 1 bonus point for a team which loses by less than 7 points
- 1 bonus point for a team which scores 4 tries or more

2-1-0 system
- 2 points for a win
- 1 point for a draw
- 0 points for a loss
- Bonus points are not applicable

In South Africa, most tournaments use the 4-2-1 system, with semi-finals and finals following.

International teams and competitions

The international team in South Africa is called the Springboks. Please note that even in English the name remains Springboks and not 'Springbucks'. They wear green-and-gold jerseys and represent South Africa in various international tournaments. The players in this team are the cream of the crop, hence they are also the highest-paid players in the country. When the national team plays against the national team of another country, the encounter is called a 'test match'.

Rugby World Cup

The biggest and most prestigious international rugby competition is called the Rugby World Cup (RWC). South Africa won the RWC competition in 1995 but surrendered it to Australia in 1999. In 2003 England came up trumps, but were defeated by South Africa who won the tournament in 2007 and are once again the current world champions. It is held once every four years and the 20 highest-ranking teams in the world at the time participate. The teams are divided into four groups, comprising five teams each. All the teams in the same group play against each other, and each group has its own log. Points are accumulated on the log using the 4-2-1 system. The two teams with the most points in each group will qualify for the quarter-finals. Teams that lose in the quarter-finals go home, leaving four teams to compete for the coveted cup. The two losing teams in the semi-finals will play against each other to determine the third and fourth places, while the two winners compete for the world championship. The World Cup trophy is called the William Webb Ellis Trophy, after the founder of the game (see Chapter 6). The winners of this tournament will be the world champions for the following four years, until the next World Cup competition. The International Rugby Board has a system by which international teams are ranked, based on their performance. The world champions may very well perform badly between World Cup tournaments and drop in their IRB rankings, but they will not lose their title as world champions until a different team wins the World Cup.

Tri-Nations

The Tri-Nations tournament is contested between New Zealand, Australia and South Africa. It takes place during July and August each year. The first Tri-Nations tournament was held in 1996, with New Zealand being the first Tri-Nations champions. South Africa won the tournament in 1998 and again in 2004. Until recently, the competition saw each team play against the other two nations twice; at home and away. In 2005 it was expanded to three games (with the exception of 2007 because of the proximity of the Rugby World Cup tournament). Again, teams accumulate log points according to the 4-2-1 system. The team with the most points on the log wins the tournament; there is no semi-final or final.

Six Nations

This is the premier rugby union championship of the northern hemisphere. This competition dates as far back as 1883. The inaugural tournament was called the Home Series and was contested between England, Scotland, Wales and Ireland. Although France played in a few friendly matches against these teams in the early 1900s, they only officially joined the Home Series in 1910 when the name of the competition was changed to the Five Nations. In 2000, the Italians joined this prestigious tournament and it has since been know as the Six Nations Championship. Each team plays once against every other team in the competition with home-ground advantage alternating from one year to the next. Points are accumulated on the tournament log based on the 2-1-0 system. The team with the most points on the log wins the championship. There are no finals or semi-finals. If one team wins all their games in one tournament, it is called a 'Grand Slam'. If one of the British teams beat all of the other 'Home Nations' (England, Ireland, Scotland or Wales) it is called the 'Triple Crown'. Trophies are also awarded for the winners of either the Grand Slam or the Triple Crown.

International Rugby Board (IRB) schedule

Over and above the Tri-Nations and Six Nations tournaments, the IRB has a schedule of international matches that happens every year. Different teams tour South Africa and play a test match or a series of test matches against the Springboks. These tours happen towards the end of May and June every year and are contested as a tournament in themselves. If there is just one test, the tournament is decided on that one game. South Africa embarks on a tour of its own during November and early December of each year, matching up with its European counterparts and Argentina, as dictated by the IRB schedule.

Regional teams and competitions

These tournaments are called 'regional', as opposed to 'provincial' because the teams are made up of a number of provincial teams combining forces to take on the regional teams from other countries and different regions in their own country.

Super 14

This tournament started in 1993, and was called the Super 10, because there were ten teams competing in the championship. The first-ever Super 10 tournament was won by the (then) Transvaal team, today known as the Lions. It then evolved into the Super 12, and is now the Super 14, because of the increasing number of teams entered into the competition. It is held annually between February and May and teams from South Africa, Australia and New Zealand participate. The winner is crowned the best regional side in the southern hemisphere. The teams in the competition are:

Team	Where are they from?
South African teams	
Bulls	Pretoria
Lions	Johannesburg
Sharks	Durban
Cheetahs	Bloemfontein
Stormers	Cape Town
Australian teams	
Waratahs	Sydney
Reds	Brisbane
Brumbies	Canberra
Western Force	Perth
New Zealand teams	
Crusaders	Christchurch
Blues	Auckland
Hurricanes	Wellington
Highlanders	Dunedin
Chiefs	Hamilton

These teams are regional teams or franchises so the cities listed are their home bases. But in reality, the players mostly come from provincial teams in the vicinity of these cities (*see* page 100 which explains how regional teams are made up). Every team plays against every other team in the tournament. They accumulate points on the log during the season according to the 4-2-1 system. Once all the teams have played against each other, the top four teams on the log will play in the semi-finals. These games will take place at the home grounds of the teams ending first and second. The team ending first will play their semi-final against the team that ended fourth on the log; the team that ended second on the log will play their semi-final against the team that ended third.

The final will be played between the two winners of the semi-finals, and at the home ground of the finalist that ended highest on the log.

Provincial teams and competitions

South Africa has the oldest domestic competition still in existence today. The competition was established in 1889. In 1892 it acquired a trophy called the Currie Cup. To this day, domestic teams in South Africa battle it out for the prestigious Currie Cup between June and October every year.

Currie Cup

The format of this competition has changed often over the years. Pre-1994, the country had four main provinces. These were Transvaal, the Orange Free State, Natal and the Cape Province. Transvaal and the Cape Province were the two biggest provinces; therefore they were each allowed to enter two teams in the Currie Cup tournament. Those teams were:

- Transvaal
- Northern Transvaal
- Free State

- Natal
- Eastern (Cape) Province
- Western (Cape) Province

After 1994, the country was divided into 14 rugby provinces, each with its own rugby team. The South African Rugby Union soon realized that a competition involving 14 different teams diluted the talent of the country as well as spectator interest in the competition, because many of the smaller unions were not competitive. They have since restructured the competition, dividing the Currie Cup into a premier division and a first division. The best eight provinces play in the Premier Division; the other six compete in a competition of their own called the First Division. The team that wins the Premier Division is crowned as the Currie Cup champions.

At the end of the season, the team that wins the First Division, and the team that ends second, will play against the two teams that ended last in the Premier Division. This is seen as a mini-tournament, and points are accumulated on a log according to the 4-2-1 system. The two teams at the top of this log will compete in the Premier Division the following year. The participating teams in the 2009 season are:

Premier Division

Team	Where are they from?
Blue Bulls	Pretoria (Tshwane)
Golden Lions	Johannesburg
Cheetahs	Bloemfontein
Sharks	Durban
Western Province	Cape Town
Griquas	Kimberley
Boland	Wellington
Leopards	Potchefstroom

First Division

Team	Where are they from?
Eagles	George
Griffons	Welkom
Mighty Elephants	Port Elizabeth
Pumas	Witbank
Valke	Brakpan
Border Bulldogs	East London

Every team plays against every other team twice; at home and away. Points are scored on the log according to the 4-2-1 system. The four teams with the most points will play in semi-final matches, and the winners of these matches will battle it out for the Currie Cup and First Division championships respectively.

The regional teams that compete in the Super 14 tournament are made up by the provincial teams combining forces. The teams are combined as follows:

Regional team	Provincial teams
Lions	Golden Lions
	Valke
Bulls	Blue Bulls
	Leopards
	Pumas
Sharks	Sharks
	Border Bulldogs
	Mighty Elephants
Cheetahs	Cheetahs
	Griquas
	Griffons
Stormers	Western Province
	Eagles
	Boland Kavaliers

Vodacom Cup

Other than being the feeding source for the regional Super 14 tournament, the Vodacom Cup championship opens the door for amateur players who are ready for the step up into the professional arena. This tournament is held between March and June annually, the same time as the Super 14 tournament. This means that players who are drafted to play for the regional sides in the Super 14 do not participate in the Vodacom Cup. Their absence creates opportunities for players from the club league or Under-21 competitions to fill their spots and to show their stuff. If the regional sides incur injuries, they will look at the Vodacom Cup team in their area for players to replace the injured. The same provincial teams who compete in the Currie Cup participate in the Vodacom Cup. The format of the competition is different to the Currie Cup structure, in that the 14 provincial teams are divided into a northern and a southern division. The teams are split up as follows:

Northern Division	Southern Division
Bulls	Free State
Valke	South Western Districts [SWD] (George)
Lions	Wildebeeste (Natal)
Pumas	Kavaliers
Griquas	Western Province
Griffons	Border
Leopards	Mighty Elephants

In this competition every team plays against every other team in their division twice; at home and away. Each division has its own log, and teams accumulate points on the log according to the 4-2-1 system. The top four teams in each division qualify to play in the quarter-finals. In the quarter-finals, teams will play against the top four teams from the other division. The winners of these games, in turn, will play in two semi-final matches. These winners will take the field to determine who are the Vodacom Cup champions.

*****

Now that you know which animal belongs in which cage, you can easily pick a team worthy of your support. Your place of residence or place of birth are obvious reasons for supporting a team, but I know that other factors—such as the physique of a certain player or the eyes of another—can easily sway a female spectator's loyalty.

Summary

- Tournaments make use of a competition log to determine the winners, or which of the teams advance to a knockout stage.

- Points are accumulated on the competition log according to the 4-2-1 system or the 2-1-0 system.

- The Rugby World Cup is the largest international rugby competition.

- South Africa won the 2007 World Cup even though they were ranked fourth for the tournament. It is held every four years, with the next one to be held in 2011 in New Zealand.

- South Africa competes annually in the following international tournaments:

  - Tri-Nations (South Africa, Australia and New Zealand)
  - IRB scheduled tour

- Regional teams are teams made up by a number of provincial teams combining forces. South Africa's regional franchises annually compete in the Super 14 competition against regional sides from Australia and New Zealand.

- Provincial teams in South Africa compete in two annual competitions:

  - Currie Cup
  - Vodacom Cup

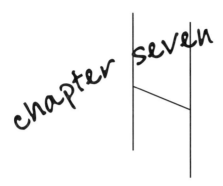

Names to drop and statistics to know

The origin of rugby

Rugby is a market town in the county of Warwickshire, situated on the River Avon in the West Midlands of England. It was at Rugby School, one of England's oldest and most prestigious public schools, where a 16-year-old boy called William Webb Ellis picked up the ball and ran with it while playing soccer in 1823. The defenders, obviously annoyed by his blatant disregard for the rules of soccer, chased him down and tackled him. From there on, this form of the game took shape and over the years it grew into the game we know today as rugby. This legend has since been debunked and it has been proven that soccer rules as we know them today did not exist at that time and that running with the ball was not uncommon. Nevertheless, his name has become immortalized by the William Webb Ellis Trophy, which is handed to the winners of the Rugby World Cup. If you ever visit the town of Rugby, look out for the plaque at the school, erected in Webb Ellis's memory:

> This stone commemorates the exploit of William Webb Ellis, who with a fine disregard for the rules of football as played in his time took the ball in his arms and ran with it, thus originating

the distinctive feature of the rugby game. AD 1823

The ten biggest rugby-playing nations in the world are, in order of ranking as at 31 October 2008:

1) New Zealand	6) Wales
2) South Africa	7) France
3) Australia	8) Ireland
4) Argentina	9) Scotland
5) England	10) Italy

Rugby World Cup statistics

With the Rugby World Cup being the most important rugby event in any supporter's diary, some key statistics have been summarized below. Armed with these nuggets of knowledge, you will be able to hold your own and even impress some of the most ardent supporters at the office! The first Rugby World Cup tournament was held in 1987.

The winners

1987	New Zealand
1991	Australia
1995	South Africa
1999	Australia
2003	England
2007	South Africa

Note: South Africa did not compete in the 1987 or 1991 World Cup tournaments because of international isolation.

Most World Cup tries

Jonah Lomu (New Zealand)	15

Rory Underwood (England)   11
David Campese (Australia)   10
Brian Lima (Samoa)   10
Gavin Hastings (Scotland)   9
Jeff Wilson (New Zealand)   9

Most tries in one World Cup tournament
Jonah Lomu (New Zealand)   8
Bryan Habana (South Africa)   8

Highest points scorers in Rugby World cups
Johnny Wilkinson (England)   243
Gavin Hastings (Scotland)   227
Michael Lynagh (Australia)   195
Grant Fox (New Zealand)   170
Andrew Mehrtens (New Zealand)   163

Springbok statistics

World Cup: winning captains
Francois Pienaar (1995)
John Smit (2007)

World Cup: winning coaches
Kitch Cristie (1995)
Jake White (2007)

Who kicked the winning drop goal in extra time of the 1995 World Cup Final?
Joel Stransky

Win ratio against:

New Zealand	40.28%
British Lions	48.84%
England	53.57%
France	55.56%
Australia	59.68%

Most consecutive wins by the Sprinboks
17 in the 1997–98 season

Most consecutive losses by the Springboks
7 in the 1964–65 season

Largest winning margin
131 points, beating Uruguay 134–3 in 2005

Largest losing margin
50 points, losing 53–3 to England in 2002

Highest points scored against the Springboks
55 points losing 55–35 to New Zealand in 1997

Most tries scored in a game
21 against Uruguay in 2005

Most tries conceded in a game
7 against New Zealand in 1997

Most points by a player in a game
34 by Jannie de Beer against England in 1999

Most tries scored by a player in a game
6 by Tonderai Chavhanga against Uruguay in 2005

Most drop goals in a game
5 by Jannie de Beer against England in 1999

Most test match appearances
102 by Percy Montgomery 1997–2008

Highest points scorer
893 by Percy Montgomery 1997–2008

Most test tries
38 by Joost van der Westhuizen 1993–2003

Most test drop goals
27 by Naas Botha 1980–1992

Captains: win ratios

Morné du Plessis	86% in 15 tests
Joost van der Westhuizen	80% in 10 tests
Gary Teichmann	72% in 36 tests
Francois Pienaar	65% in 29 tests

Note: John Smit's record is not shown here because he is the current Springbok captain. To date he has been successful in over 70% of his 54 outings as captain.

Coaches: win ratios

Kitch Christie	100% in 14 tests
Nick Mallet	71% in 38 tests
André Markgraaf	61% in 13 tests

Harry Viljoen   53% in 15 tests
Jake White   67% in 54 tests

Impressive player records

Most international tries
David Campese (Australia)   64

Most successful penalties
Neil Jenkins (Wales)   235

Highest number of international games played
George Gregan (Australia)   115

Most international points
Neil Jenkins (Wales)   1,052

Other interesting facts

Oldest game in the system
27 March 1871: Scotland 4 England 1

The highest-scoring game ever
Hong Kong 164   Singapore 13

Most consecutive wins
Argentina   20

Most consecutive losses
France   18

Most games played
France   627

Many other statistics and records exist, particularly if you want to check records within a certain tournament or if you are looking for specific players. These can be found at www.rugbydata.com

Other forms of the game

Sevens rugby

Sevens rugby has grown in stature over the last five years. Players now specialize in this form of the game, and will often not play 15-man rugby. The rules are the same as for the 15-man game; the only difference being that there are only seven players in a team—three forwards and four backs. The field is the same size as for the 15-man game hence huge space is available for individual brilliance and flair. Team strategy and game plans become less important than individual player skills at beating opponents with footwork, pace or, to a lesser extent, power. This game is ideal for the quicker players; you will seldom find a tight forward playing Sevens. Each half is only seven minutes' long. A tournament is normally held over a weekend, where each team will play several matches. Because the game focuses on individual skill rather than team strategy, you will often find nations who do not perform particularly well in the 15-man arena doing very well at Sevens. The premier tournament is called the IRB Sevens World Series. It is contested in different countries over a number of weekends during the year, the most famous tournament being the Hong Kong Sevens played in March each year. The standings of the teams in the 2007–08 series are:

1) New Zealand	6) Argentina
2) South Africa	7) Kenya
3) Samoa	8) Australia
4) Fiji	9) Wales
5) England	10) Scotland

Women's rugby

Yes, you heard right—girls can play too! The Women's Rugby World Cup has become a huge event. The rules are the same as for their male counterparts; the only difference being that the change-room doubtless smells a bit nicer, and I would imagine a bit more padding is used in strategic places! South Africa participated in the 2006 Women's World Cup, but they could not prevail against the bigger and stronger ladies from New Zealand and England. The standings after the Women's World Cup in 2006 are:

1) New Zealand	6) Scotland
2) England	7) Australia
3) France	8) Ireland
4) Canada	9) Spain
5) USA	10) Samoa

The South African women are currently ranked 12th in the world.

Rugby League

This is also a form of rugby but the rules are vastly different. The game developed while Rugby Union, as we know it, was strictly an amateur sport. Rugby League then created their own governing body, and professional contracts were given to players. This game is mostly played in Great Britain and Australia.

Australian Football League

Also known as 'Aussie Rules'. The only thing this game has in common with rugby is that it is played with an oval-shaped ball. The players wear very tight shorts and offcut shirts, which often makes me wonder how much of a contact sport it really is. This game is only played in Australia, and is almost a combination of rugby and soccer. Players do carry the ball, but points are scored by kicking the ball through upright goal-posts with no height restriction.

American Football

Also known as 'Gridiron'. Not much needs to be said here—rather obviously, the only similarities are the oval-shaped ball and that it needs to carried over the opponents' try-line to score points. Naas Botha turned out for the Dallas Cowboys in the 1980s as a specialist kicker but returned to South Africa to captain the Springboks in 1992.

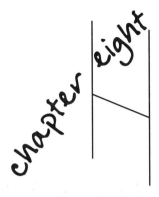

In conclusion

I have a friend who has an Australian girlfriend who recently moved to South Africa from Melbourne, where rugby is not a very big sport at all. Australian-rules football and cricket draw all the attention in this big city. She told me how he, after she had been in South Africa for about four months, asked her whether there was anything that she hadn't expected, did not like, or if there was anything he could change to make her stay here more enjoyable. She replied that she was actually rather happy, and that she was only slightly disappointed that they had to watch rugby *every* Saturday. She says the look on his face—one of complete amazement, disgust and confusion—said it all!

"I didn't mean those things."

"I was referring to things we can change."

"You obviously didn't understand what I meant!"

After a subtle throat-clearing, the subject was swiftly changed.

In South Africa, rugby is such an integral part of our culture and entertainment habits that birthday parties, weddings and even funerals are routinely scheduled around big games. Even if you are oblivious to rugby activities in this country, you are bound to be affected by it in one way or another at some stage of your life. I guess what I am saying is—if you can't beat them, join them!

You now know the basics of the game, why the whistle blows and who's who in the South African rugby arena. You will also have learned some interesting statistics which will impress even the most ardent enthusiast. Above all, if this guide has managed to encourage you to speed up a little bit in the shopping mall, it will have served its purpose.

Keep watching! It's like a new relationship ... it gets better every time you do it!

Some time ago, three Welsh friends attended the funeral of one of their best friends. Upon their return they bumped into an acquaintance of theirs, who asked about the event. The answer, spoken very softly and sincerely:

"What a beautiful sermon, led by Pastor McNeil— magnificent! Then the choir burst into song and their angelic voices mesmerized the entire congregation! After that, the wake—so wonderfully arranged by Sister Anne and her helpers ... the décor, the music and the deeply special words spoken by Jeff's brother ... a solemn affair! But then Wales lost to England in the Six Nations and it cast a gloom over the whole affair!"

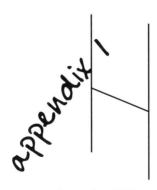

Meet the ELVs

The International Rugby Board decided to implement a set of experimental laws (Experimental Law Variations), which took effect on 1 August 2008. These laws will be tested until 1 August 2009, when a decision will be taken on the permanence or otherwise of these variations on the current laws. There are seven ELVs:

Helpie
Maulie
Scrummie
Kicky
Quicky
Liny
Cornie

Helpie

Helpie is the assistant referee. Under current rules he is called a touch-judge and his duties are limited. Prior to August 2008, he had three main duties:

- To signal when the ball, or a player carrying the ball, goes over the touch-line.
- To adjudicate whether the ball went over the crossbar and between the uprights from penalties and conversion kicks.
- To advise Reffie if he spots any foul play. Now that his name has changed to assistant referee, he helps Reffie with all his duties. He

is in radio contact with Reffie, and will let him know if he spots an infringement that Reffie didn't see. Reffie will take advice from the assistant referees, but he alone will make the final decision.

Maulie

Prior to 1 August 2008, it was illegal to deliberately collapse a maul. The concern was that it made it very hard to defend against, and there was virtually no counter. The ELV, Maulie, makes it legal to pull the maul to the ground, as long as the players are being pulled down from somewhere between their hips and shoulders.

Scrummie

Under current rules, back-line players have to be behind the feet of the last player at scrum time to be onside. Scrummie says they have to be five metres behind the last man's feet. This creates more space for attacking. Back-lines are meant to enhance the attacking opportunities from the scrum.

Kicky

This ELV has forced a rather drastic change in the defensive strategies of teams. Players would often pass the ball back to a teammate inside his 22-metre area, to kick the ball out. The fact that he was in his own 22-metre area gave him the right to kick the ball out on the full. Kicky does not allow this. The only time a player is permitted to kick the ball out on the full is if he catches it, or picks it up, inside his 22-metre area. If the ball is carried back by himself, or passed to him by a teammate outside the 22-metre area, he cannot kick the ball out on the full. If he does, the lineout will be held in line with the spot where he kicked from and not where the ball crossed the touch-line. If the ball is carried, or passed, back into the 22-metre area and the player with ball is tackled, which leads to a ruck or a maul, the ball may be kicked directly into touch once it emerges.

Quicky

This ELV refers to the quick throw-in of the ball once it has gone into touch. Previously this ball had to be thrown in straight, just like at a normal lineout. Quicky allows the quick throw-in to be legal, as long as it is thrown straight, or backwards towards the thrower's try-line.

Liny

Prior to the introduction of the ELV's, the team throwing the ball into the lineout dictated how many players formed part of the line. The defensive team had to have exactly the same number of players in the lineout, otherwise they would concede a free kick. The introduction of Liny brought about a situation where the number of players committed to lineouts was not governed. Each team can decide how many players they want to commit to the lineout, and there is no maximum number. The scrum-half, or any other player who is fulfilling that role at the lineout, has to stand at least two metres clear of the line. The non-throwing hooker is also compelled to stay two metres clear of the line until the ball has been thrown in.

Cornie

This ELV refers to the corner flag. Under current rules, a try will not be awarded if a player dives for the corner and touches the corner flag before he grounds the ball. Cornie says this ball is not out and can be played, or the try can be awarded. The only instance where the corner flag will be deemed to be out, is when a player grounds the ball on or against the flag. This also means that if a ball is kicked, hits the corner flag and is then deflected back infield, play will continue.

These following two ELVs are only being used in South Africa. However, there is every liklihood they will be implemented in the 2009 Super 14.

Freaky

Freaky is the little ELV that changed the punishment measures for certain offences. According to Freaky, penalties will be awarded for offside play as well as foul play. Any other 'penalty' infringements will be converted to free kicks. Holding on to the ball on the ground and hands in the ruck, for example, are punished with penalties under the current rules. With Freaky in the game, these offences will be punished by free kicks. In addition to converting previous penalty offences into free kicks, Freaky amends the laws at ruck time. He says that a team which carried the ball into the ruck has a couple of seconds to clear it, but failing to do so will result in a free kick to the defending team.

Tackly

This ELV creates offside lines as soon as a player is tackled. This means that other defenders will have to run around, and may only play the ball from their own side. As the laws are currently written, offside lines only come into play when the ruck is formed, i.e. when three or more players are already involved in the tackle situation.

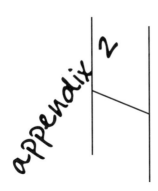

Fixtures 2009

British Lions tour of South Africa

Date	Hosts	Opponents	Venue
30 May	British Lions	Highveld XV	Royal Bafokeng, Rustenburg
3 June	British Lions	Golden Lions	Ellis Park, Johannesburg
6 June	British Lions	Cheetahs	Vodacom Park, Bloemfontein
10 June	British Lions	Sharks	Absa Park, Durban
13 June	British Lions	Western Province	Newlands, Cape Town
17 June	British Lions	Coastal XV	TBA
20 June	British Lions	Springboks	Absa Park, Durban
23 June	British Lions	Emerging Springboks	Newlands, Cape Town
27 June	British Lions	Springboks	Loftus Versfeld, Pretoria
4 July	British Lions	Springboks	Ellis Park, Johannesburg

Tri-Nations Tournament

Date	Hosts	Opponents	Venue
18 July	New Zealand	Australia	Auckland
25 July	South Africa	New Zealand	Bloemfontein
1 Aug	South Africa	New Zealand	Durban
8 Aug	South Africa	Australia	Cape Town
22 Aug	Australia	New Zealand	Sydney
29 Aug	Australia	South Africa	Perth
5 Sep	Australia	South Africa	Brisbane
12 Sep	New Zealand	South Africa	Hamilton
19 Sep	New Zealand	Australia	Wellington

Six Nations

Date	Hosts	Opponents	Venue
7 Feb	England	Italy	London
7 Feb	Ireland	France	Dublin
8 Feb	Scotland	Wales	Edinburgh
14 Feb	France	Scotland	Paris
14 Feb	Wales	England	Cardiff
15 Feb	Italy	Ireland	Rome
27 Feb	France	Wales	Paris
28 Feb	Ireland	England	Dublin
28 Feb	Scotland	Italy	Edinburgh
14 March	Scotland	Ireland	Edinburgh
14 March	Italy	Wales	Rome
15 March	England	France	London
21 March	Italy	France	Rome
21 March	Wales	Ireland	Cardiff

Super 14

Round 1: 13/14 February

Hosts	Opponents	Venue
Crusaders	Chiefs	Christchurch
Bulls	Reds	Pretoria
Stormers	Sharks	Cape Town
Lions	Cheetahs	Johannesburg
Hurricanes	Waratahs	Wellington
Highlanders	Brumbies	Dunedin
Western Force	Blues	Perth

Round 2: 20/21 February

Hosts	Opponents	Venue
Stormers	Reds	Cape Town
Sharks	Lions	Durban
Brumbies	Crusaders	Canberra
Bulls	Blues	Pretoria
Western Force	Cheetahs	Perth
Waratahs	Chiefs	Sydney
Hurricanes	Highlanders	Wellington

Round 3: 27/28 February

Hosts	Opponents	Venue
Stormers	Blues	Cape Town
Lions	Bulls	Johannesburg
Waratahs	Highlanders	Sydney
Chiefs	Sharks	Hamilton
Reds	Cheetahs	Brisbane
Crusaders	Hurricanes	Christchurch
Brumbies	Western Force	Canberra

Round 4: 6/7 March

Hosts	Opponents	Venue
Bulls	Stormers	Pretoria
Warathas	Reds	Sydney
Blues	Sharks	Auckland
Highlanders	Crusaders	Dunedin
Chiefs	Western Force	Hamilton
Hurricanes	Cheetahs	Wellington

Round 5: 13/14 March

Hosts	Opponents	Venue
Brumbies	Waratahs	Canberra
Stormers	Lions	Cape Town
Reds	Sharks	Brisbane
Highlanders	Chiefs	Dunedin
Blues	Cheetahs	Auckland
Crusaders	Western Force	Christchurch

Round 6: 20/21 March

Hosts	Opponents	Venue
Lions	Brumbies	Johannesburg
Waratahs	Crusaders	Sydney
Chiefs	Blues	Hamilton
Hurricanes	Bulls	Wellington
Highlanders	Cheetahs	Dunedin
Western Force	Sharks	Perth

Round 7: 27/28 March

Hosts	Opponents	Venue
Lions	Hurricanes	Johannesburg
Sharks	Brumbies	Durban
Reds	Chiefs	Brisbane
Crusaders	Stormers	Christchurch
Highlanders	Bulls	Dunedin
Blues	Waratahs	Auckland

Round 8: 3/4 April

Hosts	Opponents	Venue
Sharks	Hurricanes	Durban
Cheetahs	Brumbies	Bloemfontein
Waratahs	Stormers	Sydney
Crusaders	Bulls	Christchurch
Western Force	Reds	Perth
Chiefs	Lions	Hamilton

Round 9: 10/11 April

Hosts	Opponents	Venue
Cheetahs	Sharks	Bloemfontein
Waratahs	Bulls	Sydney
Blues	Lions	Auckland
Western Force	Hurricanes	Perth
Brumbies	Stormers	Canberra
Highlanders	Reds	Dunedin

Round 10: 17/18 April

Hosts	Opponents	Venue
Sharks	Crusaders	Durban
Reds	Lions	Brisbane
Brumbies	Bulls	Canberra
Hurricanes	Stormers	Palmerston North
Cheetahs	Chiefs	Bloemfontein
Blues	Highlanders	Auckland
Waratahs	Western Force	Sydney

Round 11: 24/25 April

Hosts	Opponents	Venue
Cheetahs	Crusaders	Bloemfontein
Bulls	Chiefs	Pretoria
Western Force	Lions	Perth
Blues	Reds	Auckland
Highlanders	Stormers	Dunedin
Hurricanes	Brumbies	Wellington

Round 12: 1/2 May

Hosts	Opponents	Venue
Sharks	Highlanders	Durban
Lions	Crusaders	Johannesburg
Cheetahs	Waratahs	Kimberley
Hurricanes	Blues	Wellington
Reds	Brumbies	Brisbane
Stormers	Chiefs	Cape Town
Bulls	Western Force	Pretoria

Round 13: 8/9 May

Hosts	Opponents	Venue
Lions	Highlanders	Johannesburg
Bulls	Cheetahs	Pretoria
Brumbies	Blues	Canberra
Crusaders	Reds	Christchurch
Sharks	Waratahs	Durban
Stormers	Western Force	Cape Town
Chiefs	Hurricanes	Hamilton

Round 14: 15/16 May

Hosts	Opponents	Venue
Sharks	Bulls	Durban
Reds	Hurricanes	Brisbane
Chiefs	Brumbies	Hamilton
Lions	Waratahs	TBC
Western Force	Highlanders	Perth
Blues	Crusaders	Auckland
Cheetahs	Stormers	Bloemfontein

22 May: Semi-finals
29 May: Finals

(Try not to schedule your wedding on either of these two days)

Note: At the time of writing, the Currie Cup and Vodacom Cup fixtures have not as yet been finalized.

Acknowledgments

Firstly, and most importantly, I would like to thank my sponsors, Lefatshe Technologies. From the moment I met Cheslyn and Noedine they have been committed to this project, and their unwavering support and faith in the book has been magical. Without it, this book would never have seen the light of day. Derrick, the best cartoonist in South Africa, thank you for your patience and enthusiasm throughout the production of this book. Your ability to fit in and chase tight deadlines is admirable. Thank you for bringing these characters to life! To my publishers, 30° South, thank you for agreeing to take on my work at very short notice and for giving it your very special attention. Thanks, Kerrin, for your energy and willingness to go that extra mile for this project—dealing with you has been a breath of fresh air. Thanks Chris and Gavin for turning this manuscript into the professional production it is today. It is an absolute pleasure to deal with such a professional bunch of people.

It would like to thank all my ex-teammates and professional playing acquaintances for their input and support. Thank you, Kobus, for taking the time to write the foreword. Your participation in this book means a lot. Thanks to all my friends and family for their continuing support, advice, assistance and ideas—you guys were the inspiration that kept me going. Last, but not least, a great big thank you to Paula and Jess. Your patience and unswerving faith in me, coupled with your ongoing support and encouragement, has been beyond special—a contribution I will never forget.

Jaco Louw
Johannesburg
December 2008